Ressentiment

Breakthroughs in Mimetic Theory

Edited by William A. Johnsen

Ressentiment
Reflections on Mimetic Desire and Society

Stefano Tomelleri

Michigan State University Press

East Lansing

♻ The paper used in this publication meets the minimum requirements
of ANSI/NISO Z39.48-1992 (R 1997) (Permanence of Paper).

Michigan State University Press
East Lansing, Michigan 48823-5245

Printed and bound in the United States of America.

21 20 18 17 16 15   1 2 3 4 5 6 7 8 9 10

Library of Congress Control Number: 2015936790
ISBN: 978-1-61186-184-6 (pbk.)
ISBN: 978-1-60917-471-2 (ebook: PDF)
ISBN: 978-1-62895-243-8 (ebook: ePub)
ISBN: 978-1-62896-243-7 (ebook: Kindle)

Cover and book design by Erin Kirk New
Composition by Charlie Sharp, Sharp Designs, Lansing, Michigan
Cover art © Ali Mazraie Shadi. All rights reserved.

Michigan State University Press is a member of the Green Press Initiative and is
committed to developing and encouraging ecologically responsible publishing
practices. For more information about the Green Press Initiative and the use of
recycled paper in book publishing, please visit *www.greenpressinitiative.org*.

Visit Michigan State University Press at *www.msupress.org*

Contents

Foreword by René Girard

Almost entirely ignored when alive, Nietzsche had a major role in many of the philosophical and "theoretical" infatuations of the twentieth century. Among our great intellectuals he has been the only one to serve, from time to time, as the spokesman for two extremes, whose confrontation characterized intellectual movements from the beginning to the end of the twentieth century.

Until the collapse of Nazi Germany, Nietzsche was a great thinker of right-wing radicalism. In the second half of the twentieth century, it was left-wing radicalism that claimed him. He is the celebrated predecessor of the "deconstructors," and without whom it would have been impossible for others to declare themselves the legitimate heirs of the dynasty of intellectual terrorism, who, every quarter of a century, have succeeded each other on the throne of avant-gardism.

It took until the last few years of the century to realize that Nietzsche was no longer fashionable. Today, we cannot reread his works without noting that, in actual fact, some of his theses have become out-of-date. The opposition between Apollo and Dionysus, for example, is a subject now only discussed in school-leaving examinations. Zarathustra and *Übermensch* are terribly outdated.

Well then, you ask me, why this book, why go back to Nietzsche? Wouldn't it have been better if Stefano Tomelleri had forgotten this philosopher? I don't think so, because, together with the old Nietzsche, there are ideas in his works that are incredibly topical, and in particular the one discussed in this book, ressentiment.

Ressentiment is rather an antiquated term in French and for some time has had a meaning very similar to *sentiment*. *Ressentiment* comes from the verb *ressentir*, to feel strongly, just as *sentiment* comes from *sentir*. Before Nietzsche's work, the initial *re* did not add much to the meaning of the term. Perhaps it suggested a certain persistence of the sentiment evoked, or its reappearance after being eclipsed by something else. Ressentiment was spoken of in reference to both positive feelings, such as gratitude, and negative feelings, such as hostility or the desire for revenge.

In general, the desire for revenge produces a revengeful action. But if this violence is not generated, if the desire cannot be satisfied, it has the tendency, like all desires, to endure and become even more of an irritation.

In its traditional meaning, therefore, ressentiment seems disposed, and even predisposed, to tend toward an idea of failure or a series of failures, which, by frustrating the desire, seem to reinforce it. It is probable that this tendency began even before Nietzsche, but only in draft form, and without implying that which is essential in the Nietzschean idea, that is, the *irremediable* character of failure, which is prone to having permanent effects on the personality of the victim.

We live in a world where many people, rightly or wrongly, feel blocked, or paralyzed, in all their aspirations, obstructed from achieving their most legitimate goals. Individual psychology inevitably ends up resenting this permanent frustration, and the need arises for a term that expresses this state of affairs. In French, the word *ressentiment* seems designed to play this role, to embrace the meaning that it has been finally given, not by a French writer, but by a German: Nietzsche.

At the beginning, the contribution of Nietzsche consisted of limiting the term to the realm of revenge, and later, above all, in greatly strengthening the meaning of the initial *re*, which now indicates an unsurmountable obstacle: the other, the victorious rival. It is failure that transforms the original desire into a desire for revenge, but the revenge cannot overcome this obstacle any more than the original desire, and dissatisfaction increases.

Like a wave over a rock, the desire for revenge shatters against the triumphant other and flows back toward the subject, who is left to become continuously submerged in ressentiment. The result is a very unique type of human being, who in our world proliferates to the extent that, according to Nietzsche, democratic and modern societies can be defined through him: they are the societies dedicated to ressentiment, always marked by this type of man.

Nietzsche adapted the meaning of the term *ressentiment* to the direction that suited his thoughts, but the composition of the word, the somewhat vague neutrality of the initial *re*, predisposed ressentiment to interpret the role that Nietzsche gave to it. Perhaps the linguistic genius of Nietzsche envisaged and in some way legitimized an evolution that would have occurred even without him, but, without doubt, less quickly.

Observing this mutual affinity between the term and its modern semantic evolution does not lessen Nietzsche's merits; on the contrary: it underlines his linguistic genius, which is even more remarkable in this case, in which he expresses himself in a language that is not his own.

It is surprising to discover that today in French the word *ressentiment* has lost its traditional meanings, and is used with one meaning, not always genuinely Nietzschean certainly, but at least Nietzschean in a cursory manner. In classical French the term has only one meaning, which is the same not only in German, but also in other languages, which recognize it as being a foreign word that is distinguished, according to Nietzsche, by a particular meaning. In French, even for those who do not know this story, the word has no other meanings than the one Nietzsche gave to it.

During the twentieth century, this meaning did not remain unchanged; it expanded with respect to the original definition of Nietzsche. The philosopher's error was to measure ressentiment with the rule of what he called the "will to power."

Nietzsche saw in the "will to power" a quality of being individual that, more or less, unfailingly determines the destiny of the individuals. It is what Heidegger observed: the will to power, according to Nietzsche, is *being*. Heidegger, however, didn't deduce all the consequences of this definition. For Nietzsche, those who have little will to power become necessarily the *slaves* of those who have more of it, who have *domination* engraved in their being.

What Nietzsche forgot is that, in a democratic world, relationships between individuals do not depend on the place they occupy in a mythical hierarchy of the will to power, but on a competitive mimicry, in which even the most capable are never certain that they have dominance. It is sufficient to read the painstaking work on his own will to power with a bit of good sense to understand that he unspeakably embraced the bitterest defeat, that is, ressentiment.

The discovery of ressentiment is a contribution of great importance to our knowledge, which is, unfortunately, distorted by poor Nietzsche's illusion of possessing the strongest will to power, for no other reason than it was his excellent discovery.

By default Nietzsche thought that the law of ressentiment was not valid for him. Betting everything on this certainty— and this is what he did—meant embracing, almost unerringly, defeat in real relationships with others; it meant being infected with the illness that Nietzsche despised the most: ressentiment. Nietzsche is perhaps the only one to fall into the trap that he set for his fellow humans, and his madness forms part, I think, of his genius, of his increasingly desperate battle against the verdict that his thoughts forced him to bring against himself. The truth emerges in the deranged apologies of *Ecce Homo*: "Because I am so wise, so great, so beautiful."

The most interesting aspect of ressentiment is this boomerang effect, which is terribly banal, certainly, but indisputable, and Nietzsche was clearly a victim of it. His madness was not a casual, insignificant accident, which his unquestioning admirers try to make credible. It very clearly depends on the same type of analysis that Nietzsche began, without seeing the circularity that entrapped him. In order to try to avoid the hagiographies of his unquestioning admirers, Nietzsche's discovery should be turned against himself.

Stefano Tomelleri's book is a contribution of great importance to the expansion and analysis of the Nietzschean notion of ressentiment, which is as valuable as it is dangerous. The author focuses on this idea to conduct an in-depth reflection on the true nature of human relationships. His work should be seen as a step forward of great significance toward the new science of human relationships, which has already begun to replace, in his work in particular, both sociology and psychology, and all the disciplines that are still characterized by a subjectivism and a conceptualism in decline. This research, as thorough as it is brilliant, is an important step in going beyond the views of the twentieth century.

Foreword by Paul Dumouchel

"Freedom and Resentment" is the title of a famous paper in moral philosophy by Peter Strawson.[1] The term "freedom" in the title is slightly misleading, but "resentment" is not. The paper is not really about freedom; rather, it is about the irrelevance of the debate between freedom of the will and determinism to issues in moral philosophy. Whether the thesis of determinism is true or not, argues Strawson, is of no consequence whatsoever to the propriety of our basic moral practices and concepts of condemnation, praise, indignation, punishment and desert. For these arise out of spontaneous reactive attitudes that we have toward each other's action. These reactive attitudes are constitutive of human interaction, argues Strawson. Even if they are to some extent sensitive to transformations in agents' beliefs, the way in which they are has nothing to do with the truth or falsity of determinism, and they cannot be abandoned as a whole. Interestingly, as a privileged example of these reactive attitudes, and as a form of basic proto-moral sentiment, Strawson chooses resentment.

Resentment, that is: the ill will, the negative disposition that we normally, and spontaneously, experience toward those who deliberately injured us, or simply manifested toward us contempt, a malevolent attitude, or careless indifference. A negative disposition, he adds, that may bring us to suspend the prohibition against hurting others. This reaction, says Strawson, indicates "how much we actually mind, how much it matters to us, whether the actions of other people—and particularly of *some* other people—reflect attitudes towards us of goodwill, affection or esteem on the one hand or contempt, indifference, or malevolence on the other."[2] The term "resentment," according to Strawson, refers to this reactive attitude in its "egocentric form"; that is, it corresponds to the reaction we have toward those who injured us directly. Resentment, as a basic reactive attitude, implies that we consider these others, the perpetrators of offenses toward us, as moral agents responsible for their action, at least in the sense that they intentionally committed the action. Resentment implies this, inasmuch as we will excuse offenders, spare them our resentment, if we discover that they did it by accident, or were just a child, or senile. In fact, that is precisely the way in which this reactive attitude is sensitive to changes in our beliefs. The extent of our resentment is directly related to whether or not we believe the other acted intentionally, and whether we judge that resentment is, in the case at hand, morally justified, is directly related to whether or not we believe the other acted intentionally.

However, we can also have a similar negative reaction toward offenses that are made to others. In that case this reactive attitude constitutes, according to Strawson, a strictly moral reaction, and to describe it we speak of indignation or of moral condemnation. Even if he is not very clear about this, it seems that in this case resentment is moral because the resentful agent acts in a disinterested manner; he or she has resentment on the behalf of another. The proto-moral attitude of resentment then becomes a properly moral sentiment when it becomes vicarious, when we feel offended by the offenses made to others.

Resentment, of course, is not the same thing as ressentiment, but it is related. According to Nietzsche, and also Max Scheler, ressentiment can be understood as a form of *frustrated resentment*. It is an inwardly turned negative attitude that occurs when agents are unable to express their resentment, unable to respond to the offense they have experienced. Ressentiment is failed resentment. It is not, however, failure to resent, for Nietzsche and Scheler, like Strawson, think that resentment is a spontaneous reactive attitude that is constitutive of human interactions. It is the failure to carry out, to formulate, or to act upon one's resentment that gives rise to ressentiment. In consequence, ressentiment, unlike resentment, is not only what philosophers call an "occurring emotion," an immediate reaction, but it is also a long-term disposition that settles in and establishes itself as a fundamental trait of character, which progressively poisons the agent's soul. For ressentiment does not arise out of just any type of failure to react or to avenge an offense, as when the perpetrator ran away and escaped, but only when this incapacity reflects the agent's weakness, his or her fear, or inability to face or to resist the offender. Ressentiment is a disease of the weak, who resent their own inferiority. It distorts their value system and makes them claim that they prefer forgiveness to revenge, or equality to hierarchy, when forgiveness is but a means to avenge themselves of those who are stronger, and equality a way to belittle those who are superior. Ressentiment disguises the truth of its own resentment; it lies to itself and to others. These false representations, the misrecognition that is at the heart of ressentiment, according to Nietzsche and Scheler, can and has changed the world. It instituted a new social, cultural, and religious order, characterized by equality, democratic rights, and humanitarian sentiments, by care for the weak and for victims. These sentiments, however, are not as virtuous as they pretend to be. They are secretly animated by failed resentment. They constitute the revenge of the weak, of the losers. Nietzsche was not described as a *maître du soupçon*, a master of suspicion, for nothing; he uncovers hidden behind our democratic and humanitarian self-satisfaction, behind Christian charity and forgiveness, a profound moral failing that belies our claims to moral superiority.

Nietzsche's and Scheler's reflections on ressentiment, argues Tomelleri, raise a formidable double moral challenge, to which we need to respond. First, to what extent are they right? Is it really the case that the modern world has been fashioned by resentment, that its fundamental moral and political categories, like equality, democracy, and rights, and its major religious ideals, like forgiveness and charity, have been shaped by hidden resentment? If it is true, what does it entail? What are the consequences of this "discovery"? This brings us to the second dimension of the challenge. Nietzsche and Scheler have transformed ressentiment into an accusation that delegitimizes moral claims. They have taught us that any claim that is motivated by ressentiment is void of all moral authority. Again, is this true? Is it really the case? Clearly the meaning we should give to the fact that some of our basic moral categories have been shaped (at least partly) by ressentiment depends on the answer we will give to that second question. The two questions then are closely linked, and interdependent, but they are different.

Tomelleri first shows that Scheler, in spite of his explicit claim to be refuting him, actually took over from Nietzsche the conceptual structure he had imposed upon the idea of ressentiment. Scheler, like Nietzsche, views ressentiment as a sign of weakness and considers that the morals it guides conceal a hidden desire for revenge, harbor envy that fails to express itself directly. The main difference between them is that while Nietzsche considers Christianity to be an expression of ressentiment, Scheler views that as a mistake and considers bourgeois morality to be its prime representative. Thus the candidates for ressentiment are not of the same social types according to both authors, Christians according to Nietzsche, bourgeois for Scheler; however, they share for both the same moral and psychological type. Ressentiment is characteristic of weak and morally immature individuals. There is more: Scheler and Nietzsche consider, as Strawson does, that resentment is a healthy reaction, but, unlike him, they do not consider this reaction to be a moment in an interrelation. Nietzsche in particular understands revenge in the context of the relation between the avenger and him- or herself, as a form of self-affirmation whose goal is to reestablish the individual as what he or she fundamentally is. It is only in the case of ressentiment that Nietzsche sees the reactive behavior as interrelational and as essentially *reactive*. Ressentiment, unlike revenge, is construed as a relation to another, a superior person whom we fear and who frustrates us of our revenge. That is precisely why ressentiment is considered an inadequate, morally inferior, attitude, because it is seen as a relation of dependence, more precisely because for Nietzsche all forms of interdependence are reduced to dependence.

Following Girard, Tomelleri argues that Nietzsche's, and Scheler's, concept of ressentiment transforms what is a moment within a social relation into an essence, into an intrinsic characteristic of certain individuals, those who are weak. In the mimetic rivalries that structure our lives we all experience failure and frustration; we all have the occasion to be weak and to become resentful. Ressentiment should not be construed as a disposition particular to some individuals, those who are weak, but as an attitude to which we are all subject at times.

However, Nietzsche and Scheler are right, argues Tomelleri, when they view ressentiment as a typically modern emotion that is closely linked to the development of equality and to democratic institutions. Building both on Nietzsche and on Girard's analyses in *Deceit, Desire, and the Novel*, Tomelleri sketches a sociology of ressentiment whose objective is to take stock of our new anthropological condition, initiated by Christian revelation. Ressentiment, he argues, is closely related to the particular moment that we are living in the process of secularization, in the slow historical transformation from societies where victims are sacred, to societies where they are innocent and where the position of the victim can be exploited for one's own advantage. "Playing the victim" is one of the forms that ressentiment takes in a globalized world where the unifying power of the nation-state is dwindling. This sociology of ressentiment constitutes the answer to the first of the two questions raised earlier: to what extent are Nietzsche and Scheler right in their analysis of ressentiment, to what extent are modern democratic institutions involved in ressentiment? Nietzsche and Scheler are right to point to the centrality of ressentiment, for it is one of the major forms that mimetic desire takes in the modern world. They are wrong in that they fail to recognize that ressentiment is essentially relational, mimetic, and view it as an essence, as a failure that is characteristic of some individuals only. They are right in that they perceive the close relationship that exists between ressentiment and Christian revelation, but they fail to understand exactly how the two phenomena are related to each other.

Beyond that sociology which analyzes the relationship between ressentiment and the transformation of sacrificial institutions initiated by Christian revelation, Tomelleri does something even more important: he answers the second question. In his answer, he completely demystifies ressentiment, or to put it in a better way: he licenses ressentiment and gives us the freedom to be *ressenti*. He argues that ressentiment, really, is not such a dirty word. When reading Nietzsche and Scheler on ressentiment, it is clear that both authors are resentful of ressentiment. They hate it; they reject it entirely, and are convinced that it has nothing to do with them. In Girard's language, they are scandalized by ressentiment, that is, both attracted and repulsed by it. This "scandal" makes possible a mimetic reading of Nietzsche's and Scheler's analyses that argues that their concept of ressentiment is itself an expression of ressentiment. Mimetic theory shows that they participate in the very process they denounce. To some extent this is Tomelleri's analysis, but to a limited extent only. More precisely, he consciously avoids the one-upmanship temptation that is inherent in such readings. Perhaps because he was, so to speak, "raised" with mimetic theory, he takes such an analysis for granted and does not consider that it constitutes, or can be reduced to, a move against Nietzsche and Scheler whose objective would be to delegitimize what they have to say. He avoids, in other words, mimetically reproducing their claim that ressentiment delegitimizes all moral claims that are tainted by it.

There is, argues Tomelleri, no need to be scandalized by ressentiment. Not that ressentiment is good, but it is ambiguous, and its ambiguity is that of mimetic desire itself, which we cannot dismiss from our life. It provides occasions of conflict and baseness, ressentiment can fuel violence, discord and injustice, but it can also open opportunities for growth, for justice, and for inventing institutions that are better adapted to the transformations of our new anthropological condition at a time when traditional means of protection against violence are disappearing, when politics is losing its sacred aura, and when vain attempts are being made to sacralize religions anew.

Freedom and ressentiment are our lot. That is, freedom from ressentiment and freedom through ressentiment, and freedom we will only keep if we do not turn ressentiment into our scapegoat. That is the central lesson of this remarkable little book that challenges our beliefs and certainty.

Acknowledgments

This book is the fruit of long conversations, reflections, and study over the course of about fifteen years of research shared with my mentor and friend Sergio Manghi. I am particularly grateful to him.

Paul Dumouchel encouraged and helped me in the crucial analytical passages. I have been truly enlightened by his comments. Not only did he help me in the initial stages of conceiving the book, but he also provided valuable assistance in completing the work.

René Girard is the main inspiration for the ideas developed in the following pages. His generous willingness to discuss personally the initial project and his scholarship were vital for me.

I must also thank those who over the years helped me by discussing the ideas and topics that I address in the book. For their attention and competence, my heartfelt thanks go to Suyen Angiolini, Roberta Bova, Vincenzo Cesareo, Martino Doni, Chiara Giaccardi, Mauro Magatti, Roberto Lusardi, and the students and colleagues of the University of Bergamo.

Introduction

That stroke of genius of Christianity—God's
sacrifice of himself for the guilt of human beings,
God paying himself back with himself, God as
the only one who can redeem man from what for
human beings has become impossible to redeem—
the creditor sacrifices himself for the debtor, out of
love (can people believe that?), out of love for his
debtor!

—Nietzsche, *The Genealogy of Morals*

This book has been written in response to Friedrich Nietzsche's provocative question that has been chosen as the epigraph of this introduction: how much and how does ressentiment condition our daily life?[1]

The decision to focus on the contemporary "experience" of ressentiment arises from three assumptions: desire and the emotional dimension of human action are crucial to understanding social interactions;[2] "social questions" are intimately linked to individual biographies via affective relationships,[3] the concrete manifestation of behavior; and the rational evaluation of costs and benefits has a role that, significantly, is always regulated by the grammar of the emotions and sentiments embodied into rituals, habits, and routines.[4]

The emotional experience of each person, in this period of increasing, often chaotic, differences, is obviously not reducible to a single tone. There are many different emotional nuances that range from disquiet to insecurity, to fear, to indifference, to the upstart's frenzy, overbearing arrogance, the forced and packaged cheerfulness of salespeople and of course, less frequently, often more briefly, we are able to obtain a space for joy, for hope, for the pleasure of sharing our existence with others.

Why should we therefore focus only on ressentiment? The response that gave rise to this book is basically this: because this emotion is truly representative of the distinctive cipher of feeling in the late-modern period, which oscillates schizophrenically between an exaggerated and narcissistic desire of individual affirmation and a sentiment of deep and radical sadness. It represents the most significant difference between the affective experience of modernity and that of the eras that preceded it, an emotive cipher to measure the entire gamut of modern and late-modern emotions, however numerous and varied these emotions may be.

During the twentieth century, we witnessed veritable eruptions of this insidious evil, and we are still witnesses of the proliferation of new forms of ressentiment at the various levels of social, family, local, and planetary life. This book aims to explore the anthropological and social assumptions that make up this evil and to explore its genesis.

The question that opens this introduction, "A society full of ressentiment?," is an explicit reference to Nietzsche's now classic work on modern morality that was subsequently critically reworked by Max Scheler.[5]

Nietzsche hypothesizes that the basic egalitarian tendency that is typical of modernity is the result of the affirmation of the Christian God, which triggered the process of dismantling the archaic sacred order that is known as secularization. Christ denounced all forms of sacrifice by protesting His innocence. In this way, He revealed the inseparable link between ritual violence and the sacred "Dionysian" harmony sanctioned by myths in all parts of the world.

Nietzsche shows what many had ignored for a long time before him, namely that it was the revelation of the Gospels that promoted this egalitarian tendency that leads to the denunciation of privileges, to the institution of civil and human rights, to democracy.[6] This reading of Western history has a tragically negative significance for Nietzsche: modern human beings have freed themselves from the symbolic order of myths and rites only to deliver themselves to a social order governed by mediocrity, envy of the stronger by the weakest, and by universal ressentiment. The egalitarian requirement of modernity, which requires our neighbor be increasingly similar to us, and which reacts with inner disappointment and a sense of injustice to any minimally excessive distinction of our neighbor, is motivated by an unacknowledged desire for revenge.[7]

The principles and rights of equality, solidarity, humanity, all Western democratic institutions, are, according to Max Scheler, the embodiment of the desire for vendetta disguised as love by people who are incapable of winning an open contest with the other. Modern humanitarianism is the new face of the ancient ressentiment of individuals who are incapable of emancipating themselves from their servility.

According to Nietzsche, the cultural transformations brought about by Christian revelation are merely an organic and systematic *justification* of ressentiment, of our weaknesses and of our mediocrity as weak people. Modern institutions hobble the will to power, fostering the proliferation of weak people.

This way of conceiving ressentiment leads Nietzsche to condemn Christian revelation for ennobling the "last," the weakest. The accusation of bestowing the same dignity on the weak as on vigorous men, of making "slave morality" triumph, producing only the destructive effect of weakening the will to power of all of humanity. Nietzsche's lesson is of enormous importance: it throws down a challenge to social scientists that cannot be ignored.[8]

Nietzsche clearly exposes the dark side of modern

democratic principles: the hypocrisy of false egalitarianism and false humanitarianism. The latter can always be used to disguise a desire for revenge on those who seem stronger than us. This is because no one, not even the most apparently mild person, is free from feelings of hate and vendetta. The analysis of the link between ressentiment and modern transformations shows that the principles of equality always risk justifying feelings of hate, envy, and bitter rivalry.

When Nietzsche condemns Christian revelation without appeal, he also delegitimizes the symbolic and institutional orders that are rooted in Christian revelation, as he himself points out. Nietzsche's model asserts that there is a complete, automatic, and necessary *coincidence* between being on the side of the weak and being part of a culture, of a morality, of a society of ressentiment; this model seems to rule out any possibility of appeal to the principles of equality, solidarity, and brotherly love because of their presumed fatal collusion with our fragility, our failures, our mediocrity, with our ressentiment, in a word.

Rising to this Nietzschean provocation also obliges modernity to address the gravity of the extreme conclusions that Nietzsche draws, that is, the judgment that secularization, with all the principles and rights that have led to modernity, is to be *condemned morally* because it justifies our ressentiment.

Our investigation accepts that *both* challenges must be taken up: the challenge of never diverting our gaze from our human baseness and the challenge of not forgetting the extreme and antidemocratic consequences that arise from limiting oneself to the Nietzschean condemnation of such lowness.

In the twentieth century, this question received scant attention from scholars. Although it is a problem of crucial importance, many studies still have to be carried out, especially at the level of empirical research, before we can define a sociology of ressentiment. In the last thirty years, we have, however, witnessed a change of course and a return to a wide series of questions that the first pioneering studies drew to public attention. The research in this field has increased constantly.[9] My hope is that this book can also contribute to deepening our understanding of this specifically late-modern emotion.

• • •

The book is divided into three parts. In the first, I have attempted to reconstruct the configuration of ideas and of values that defines the image of ressentiment according to Nietzsche, as well as in Scheler's critique of Nietzsche. The terrain on which the analysis is conducted is not so much, or not only, a historical terrain, but above all a theoretical and epistemological terrain. The main theoretical operation highlights the fact that the image of ressentiment traced by Nietzsche arises from an idea of emotions as individual and private phenomena that expose themselves to the influence of the other only as signs of immaturity and weakness.

My aim is to show that this very conception of ressentiment itself arises from the process that leads to ressentiment. Scheler partly understood this, but he did not succeed in fully developing his intuition because he was too influenced by Nietzsche's "individualistic" interpretation. Scheler undertook to demonstrate that Nietzsche's thesis is false: according to him, ressentiment is not at all the origin of Christianity. Nevertheless, when he analyzes the phenomenology of the ressentiment among modern people, he recognizes the intrinsic validity of the Nietzschean model and falls into the error that ressentiment involves only a particular category of people: bourgeois philanthropists.

In the second part of the book, I attempt to create guidelines for a relational and social model of ressentiment. This objective is not easy to attain, and the cornerstone on which I have built my model is a work that has profoundly marked contemporary anthropological and sociological thought: René Girard's mimetic theory.[10]

Choosing this theory comes from the fact that Girard, more than anyone else, has wondered about the crucial node that Nietzsche has scrutinized for ressentiment, that is, the relationship between the foundations of social order and desire.[11] By emphasizing the *desiring* dimension of the human condition and searching it for the fundamental characteristics of the relationships that inform our social life, René Girard has thrown light on the social and anthropological warp and weft of the human condition in general and of the processes of affirmation of modern institutions.[12]

Specifically, in the mimetic theory of the scapegoat René Girard has reworked the scapegoat theme in an anthropological and relational sense. He traces the origin of ressentiment to the imitative dynamics of desire, showing its dynamic, circular, and ambivalent dimension. Desire is always the desire to be like the other. Each subject desires because of his or her inadequate nature and tends to imitate the behavior of others. The vital pulsation of desire is not important, and neither is the force of attraction of certain objects; what is important is the incessant mimetic dynamism of our face-to-face interactions. Ressentiment is a historical and sophisticated form of desire that, after trying out the different possibilities of self-realization, is condemned to rivalry for its own sake.

Girard takes up what Durkheim had already sensed in *The Elementary Forms of Religious Life*.[13] He maintains that the first human communities channeled potentially competing desires through sacred rituals. Unlike the great French sociologist, Girard emphasizes the role and function of the sacrificial victim. The pacifying mechanisms of the scapegoat process, according to Girard, were very effective in maintaining order. Nevertheless, over the last two millennia they have become less and less effective because of the

Christian revelation, which has subverted the pagan sacred order. As a consequence of these radical transformations, the ancient solution that conflicts can be settled through the ritual killing of a victim is now unavailable. The final result of this sentiment of frustration produces ressentiment, the final term in the evolution of mimetic desire.

This theoretical basis makes it possible to delineate a genealogy of ressentiment that is based on the *relational* condition of our affective life, enabling us to abandon individualistic psychology in general and an individualistic notion of ressentiment in particular.[14] Girard's theory allows our deep opening to the other to be recognized, an opening to others that human nature manifests in all its aspects, positive and negative. More precisely, this part of the book tries to develop the relational and social theory of the emotions that is implicit in Girard's mimetic theory, an approach to emotions that marks the theoretical transition that is indispensable for our critical rereading of the Nietzschean idea of ressentiment.

Girard's theory is discussed only in this second part of the book, but it constitutes in fact the main inspiration of the whole work. This theory provides the social scientist with a fruitful field of research that starts with recognizing in the Judeo-Christian revelation of the fundamental role of the scapegoat as the original matrix of social transformations that are still taking place. It offers the tools required for recognizing in our fragility the human dignity revealed by the message of the Gospels.

Grasping the essential meaning of this research may be a great help, not just for understanding the social phenomena of contemporary society but also for learning to love our modern institutions, the world of rights, of justice, but without ever losing sight of their ambiguous underground, which Nietzsche, more than anyone, brought to light.

From this point of view, the institutions that are based on the principles of equality represent an institutional approach that recognizes and at the same time contains the ressentiment of modern human beings but without resorting to exclusion and expulsion, unlike what occurred in the institutions of archaic mythical ritual orders. The principle of equality and the world of rights heralded by modernity are attempts to acknowledge the profound ambivalence of every human affective experience by assigning the same *dignity* to each such affective experience, ressentiment included.

What Nietzsche failed to appreciate in Christian revelation is the fact that Christ's message, beyond its religious implications, provided people with the chance of a *new* way of becoming reconciled with one another. It is correct to define this way as new because it leaves people no excuse for justifying the violence that they do to each other, because it does not recognize that any morality, whether the most Christian and altruistic morality, or an aristocratic and individualistic morality, should consider itself to be "without sin," that is to say without ressentiment. Ressentiment thus becomes an emotional experience that individuals experience daily in mutual comparisons that no longer have any external or higher yardstick, which Nietzsche was still seeking.

The anthropological novelty of the Christian message consists of an invitation to recognize mutual dependency as a latent structure of social and human interactions. Or rather, as Girard writes, it consists in the invitation to recognize mutual imitation as a constituent form of inter-personal and social dynamics, both when these dynamics have a mythical-ritual form based on the recurrent sacrifice of a scapegoat by the community and when they take the modern democratic form that is based on the difficult renunciation of the reassurances of myth, ritual, and the scapegoat; a renunciation that may finally be impossible and is certainly always incomplete, and that has to be continu-ously repeated, through constant self-criticism. From this perspective, the close link between ressentiment and mo-dernity highlighted by Nietzsche and taken up by Scheler continues to be a scientifically fruitful tool for analyzing the processes taking place in modern society. Nevertheless, this does not automatically lead to the democratic process being declared anathema; paradoxically this close link between ressentiment and modernity reinforces the foundations of modern democracy. According to Girard, democracy is the only type of order to have emerged in human history up until now that is able to accept its own dark side as a constituent, even as a generative part and not as a foreign body to be labeled as pathological and that must accordingly be amputated, expelled, or marginalized, in accordance with mythical-magical scapegoat tenets.

In the third part of the book, we defend the hypothesis that the current feeling of endemic crisis is due to the ineffectiveness of modern instruments of self-regulation of ressentiment.

The spread of ressentiment has in particular intensified with the decline of the welfare state.[15] The horizon of sense in which we live is increasingly orientated toward offering limitless choices, but societies are by definition unable to foster the conditions that are necessary for realizing these. Increasingly ambitious desire clashes with a reality that is selective and does not always provide solidarity. Individual lives are exposed to increasing mimetic competition, to a progressive loss of the safeguards guaranteed by the system of social services of the nation-state and the traditional ways of interpreting action. In other words, the general and institutional criteria for social action and security are withering away.

In recent years, the job insecurity caused by market competition is, as in the past, the main source of uncertainty about the future and of uncertainty about social position and self-esteem that obsess citizens. The welfare state tried to protect its citizens above all from this uncertainty, by making work more secure and the future more guaranteed. This is no longer the case today. The modern state cannot anymore keep the promises of the welfare state, and it is no longer in governments' interests to renew this promise. Their policies, on the contrary, preannounce a life that will be more precarious and full of risks, and will require great skill in improvisation while making long-term planning, let alone life plans, impossible.[16] It is this "more precarious and risk-filled life" in which long-term planning has become literally impossible that endemically fills social players with the feeling of individual frustration and revenge that we call ressentiment.

1

The Revolt of the Slaves
at the Masters' Banquet

> Yea, all kings shall fall down before him: all nations
> shall serve him. For he shall deliver the needy when
> he crieth; the poor also, and him that hath no
> helper. He shall spare the poor and needy, and shall
> save the souls of the needy. He shall redeem their
> soul from deceit and violence: and precious shall
> their blood be in his sight.
>
> —Psalm 72 (King James Version)

In the preface to *The Genealogy of Morals*, Friedrich Nietzsche announced that he had discovered a new general trend in the modern era that could become a great hazard for humankind, the beginning of the end of humankind. Humankind risks embarking on an unprecedented self-destructive decline, Nietzsche writes: "It was precisely here that I saw the great danger to humanity, its most sublime temptation and seduction—seduction to what? to nothingness?—in these very instincts I saw the beginning of the end, stability, the exhaustion that gazes backwards, the turning *against* Life, the last illness announcing itself with its own mincing melancholy: I realized that the morality of pity . . . was the most sinister symptom of our modern European civilization."[1]

The great danger is allegedly caused by a symptom of regression hidden behind a formidable conspiracy orchestrated by "worthless people" against successful victorious people: the rebellion of the slaves.

For centuries, some prototypes of people, namely ill, weak, ordinary people, have been hidden in the underground of the world, where they have been silent victims of all kinds of offense and humiliation. In the meantime, however, an evil flower, the beginning of the end, was germinating in the hidden corners of that underground. That flower was ressentiment. Driven by the reactive force[2] of ressentiment, common people, slaves, those who have always been subaltern—living in prostration—were going to rebel, raising up their heads.

Nietzsche argues that this rebellion has an ancient history. The revolt began with the people of Israel, who have always been trapped in their history as victims, and could not take revenge on their persecutors, so that they had feelings of hatred and held grudges that allegedly gave rise to the first stirrings of a long rebellion.

Christian love is the culmination of this story of revenge that was never carried out. For Nietzsche, the figure of Christ both embodies and prefigures the revenge of the weak, of the oppressed who are unable to avenge themselves, of those, in other words, who are fragile. These people, after abandoning the cupboard and cellars of the world of the masters, have finally taken to the streets with Christ in order to seek revenge, calling their revenge "forgiveness."

Nietzsche believes that the new and most destructive aspect of the revenge of Judeo-Christian morality, where hatred is clothed as its opposite, lies in the fact that in the modern age revenge has assumed secular forms. Ressentiment first disguised itself as love for one's enemy, as compassion and the spirit of self-sacrifice, and thereby disguised people's egoism as purported altruism, and then transformed itself into humanitarianism and into solidarity; that is to say, it transformed itself into the world of rights that modernity has opened up. In other words, the transformations taking place in the modern age are secular forms of Christianity, and for this very reason according to Nietzsche they are an evil flower germinating from the ressentiment of mediocre people and a justification of their unfulfilled desire for revenge. Nietzsche wonders whether one does not need to seek the root of modern transformations in that general new trend characterized by the spread of ressentiment, a symptom of regression that is inherent in the good. The veritable life force of the underground that is the foundation of the bright edifices of modernity is the dark side of Christian secularization and of the resulting principles of equality, solidarity, and democracy.

The Reaction of the Weakest

In *The Genealogy of Morals*, Nietzsche placed the creative action of ressentiment at the center of the processes of secularization that are typical of the modern age, raising this emotional condition to the level of a theoretical tool as the key to understanding the social, institutional, and cultural transformation taking place in the modern era.[3] According to Sergio Moravia,[4] the program of *The Genealogy of Morals* consists of a historical reconstruction of the genesis of morals through legal-social and psychosocial and psychoanthropological paradigms, that is, from an elementary analysis of the economic, anthropological, and social elements that have contributed to the construction of morals (for example, Nietzsche derives the moral concept of guilt from the economic concept of debt). Moravia's reading of this process does not assign a crucial role to ressentiment, whereas I consider ressentiment to be the linchpin of Nietzsche's investigation into the genesis of morals.

In this work, Nietzsche carries out a systematic analysis of ressentiment and of the socioanthropological aspects of its link with the Judeo-Christian tradition. One can summarize the distinguishing marks of the Nietzschean model of ressentiment in three nodal points: the prototype of the weak-reactive people, the explosive force, and the process of subversion brought about by Christianity.

THE PROTOTYPE OF THE WEAK-REACTIVE PEOPLE

From the very beginning of *The Genealogy of Morals*, Nietzsche stresses that there is a substantial difference between the morals of masters and the morals of slaves. He emphasizes that the morals of slaves are heteronomous and "reactive," because they always stand in need of impulses coming from outside to be able to define themselves.

Nietzsche suggests that these morals originate from an open contrast between two prototypes (or also classes, or "races") of people: masters and slaves.[5] According to Giametta, *The Genealogy of Morals* can be compared with Karl Marx's *Manifesto of the Communist Party*. Just as the latter is based on the opposition between classes, Nietzsche's work is based on the contrast between prototypes: active and reactive, noble and ignoble, aristocratic and plebeian, "with the difference that Marx takes the side of the proletariat, whereas Nietzsche takes the part of the active prototype (class, race).... But he also makes the same atomistic mistake of taking it for granted that such an opposition and division between elements is simple, clear, and fixed."[6]

The masters are supposed to be founders of morals that are originative, that is, that are the product of the masters' will to power, which is based on "fullness," "force," "will to life," the masters' "bravery" and their "trust" in the "future." The slaves are supposed to have promoted the morals of ressentiment, which was at first a strategy followed by way of self-defense in order to react to the power of the former: "He [the slave] has conceived of 'the evil enemy,' the 'evil one,' and indeed that is the root idea from which he now evolves as a contrasting and corresponding figure a 'good one'—himself—his very self!"[7]

On the other hand, the morals of the nobles are established through autonomous and "active" forms: noble human beings, people of power first and foremost, define themselves and their own actions as "good" and *consequently* define as vulgar and plebeian the people and actions that are opposed to them.

This difference between counterfeit and autonomous morals arises, according to Nietzsche, from this historical emergence of a specific prototype of human being, who is characterized by a specific way of being in the world: the human being of ressentiment, a fragile and underground human being who loves to hide, a slave who is incapable of avenging himself. Nietzsche writes: "His soul squints; his mind loves hidden crannies, tortuous paths and back doors, everything secret appeals to him as his world, his safety, his balm; he is past master in silence, in not forgetting, in waiting, in provisional self-deprecation and self-abasement."[8]

This type of human being does not have an authentic existence and has no part in the profound meanings of life. According to Nietzsche, they are people who are devoid of identity, who are ready to obey any master, follow any flag. They are people who are comfortably in thrall to serving and subservience. And it is the very fragility of these people, their intrinsic weakness and lowness, that generates in their soul the "reaction" of ressentiment, that most dangerous "blasting stuff and explosive force" (Samuel translation of 1913) against the noble and the strong.

THE EXPLOSIVE FORCE

The destructive force of ressentiment is nothing other than a desire for revenge nurtured by these weak people against the strong people: an "evil" desire for revenge hidden even to themselves that in their arguments and moral justifications usurps the name of "good" justice. Nietzsche writes:

> This plan [ressentiment] blooms at its prettiest . . . ,
> a hidden flower, as it has ever been, like the violet,
> though, forsooth, with another perfume. And as
> like must necessarily emanate from like, it will not
> be a matter for surprise that it is just in such circles
> that we see the birth of endeavours . . . to sanctify
> *revenge* under the name of *justice*—as though
> Justice were at bottom merely a development of
> the consciousness of injury and thus with the

rehabilitation of revenge to reinstate generally and collectively all the *reactive emotions*.[9]

One figure who is representative of this prototype of people who are skillful in nurturing their desire for revenge is Socrates, according to Nietzsche. Socrates is the prototype of decadence, who chooses irony, dialectics, as the last resource of someone who has no other weapon with which to combat his enemy and impose his own desire to act like a tyrant. Nietzsche writes:

> Is Socratic irony an expression of revolt? of plebeian *ressentiment*? As the member of an oppressed group did Socrates take pleasure in the ferocity with which he could thrust his syllogistic knife? Did he avenge himself on the nobles he fascinated? As a dialectician, you have a merciless tool in your hands; dialectics lets you act like a tyrant; you humiliate the people you defeat. . . . The dialectician *undermines* his opponent's intellect.—What? Is dialectics just a form of *revenge* for Socrates?[10]

Socrates was a plebeian, one of the common people, a typical delinquent; he was *décadent*. The incarnate decadence of Socrates, according to Nietzsche, is closely linked to the tragic transition from the noble and sacrificial order to the plebeian and democratic order of the polis,[11] where rationality is at the same time the exorcising of the will to power and its full implementation.[12] According to Jean-Pierre Vernant and Pierre Vidal-Naquet,[13] the appearance of tragedy at the end of the sixth century BC and its subsequent disappearance just a hundred years later reflect the need of Athenian society to address the problem of the transition from a mythical and sacrificial order to a legal order. As law became established in the Greek world, it colored at the same time aspects of other social institutions, of human behavior and categories of thought in a way that was antithetical to the previous sacrificial order. On the basis of these historical premises it is possible to document and confirm the correctness of Nietzsche's philosophical and philological hypothesis that the figure of Socrates symbolizes the definitive imposition of a legal and political order.

The movement from the social order of the nobles to the morals of the slaves constituted for Nietzsche a veritable subversion of morals. The result of this profound subversion is Christian morality. Christian morality is for Nietzsche the result of a gradual process of subversion of the original aristocratic morals, brought about by the weak and the ignoble, intoxicated by ressentiment toward the strong and the noble. The Judeo-Christian tradition heralds the revenge of the weak, of the oppressed, of the fragile people, of all those who are unable to assert themselves with their own force, but who by embracing Christianity aspire to victory over the "evil enemy." According to Nietzsche, Christian love and the resulting call to pardon one's enemy disguise the "fear to avenge oneself" under the mask of "I don't want to avenge myself."

In *The Genealogy of Morals* Nietzsche draws the essential lines of a configuration of ideas and values that supply a clear theoretical model of the link between ressentiment and Christian secularization. Ressentiment is treated as an emotive condition with deeply negative connotations because it is closely connected to a certain prototype of mediocre individuals that the figure of Christ has ennobled by giving them the same dignity as other humans. Ressentiment is the emotional reaction, the revolt of the "sufferers against the sound and the victorious": it clothes itself in compassion, love, and the thirst for justice, but behind these vestments of Christian goodness there is the *reaction* of the weakest, their desire for revenge that has been buried over time. Nietzsche writes of the human being who is full of ressentiment: "While every aristocratic morality springs from a triumphant affirmation of its own demands, the slave morality says 'no' from the very outset to what is 'outside itself,' different from itself and not itself: and this *no* is its creative act. This volteface of the valuing standpoint . . . is typical of *ressentiment* . . . its action is fundamentally a reaction."[14]

This *reactive* nature of ressentiment plays a crucial part in its Nietzschean definition. According to Gilles Deleuze, the link between the explosive and deflagrating force of ressentiment and its reactive nature is a crucial theoretical key to understanding Nietzsche's thought. Deleuze's reading of Nietzsche's works, which many scholars consider to be the most faithful, illustrates the broad explanatory scope that Nietzsche attributes to the notion of ressentiment in the sense of reactive force.

The Crisis of the Will to Power

Gilles Deleuze judged *The Genealogy of Morals* to be Nietzsche's most "systematic" work. Since *Human, All Too Human*, one of the aspects at the center of Nietzsche's philosophy had been the analysis of modern prejudices in relation to the secularization of Christianity arising with modern transformations. According to Deleuze, in *The Genealogy of Morals* this topic, which is illuminated by a "*fundamental desire* for knowledge," finds its most mature and systematic expression.[15] Deleuze places ressentiment at the center of Nietzsche's philosophical speculation; the main interpretive criterion that he uses to explain its meaning is the distinction between "active forces" and "reactive forces" that Heidegger had already emphasized.

In Deleuze's interpretation, the "active forces" correspond to the will to power and the "reactive forces" to ressentiment. Deleuze's interpretive objective is to isolate the "active force" from contamination by the "reactive force" to highlight the differences in the relationship between these two vital forces.

The "active force" is a passionate vital force that leads the strong and noble human being to act autonomously and harmoniously. By contrast, the "reactive force" is a force whose source is found only externally, that leads the weak human being to act passively, in an underground and heteronomous manner. According to Deleuze, all relational, normative, community, and social activities depend for Nietzsche on the reactive forces of ressentiment, while the will to power is the sole active and true force of "desiring production" that "dispenses sense" to human actions.

According to Deleuze, the main difference between "active forces" and "reactive forces" is ascertained by reviving Nietzsche's distinction between the master and slave type because "what counts for Nietzsche is not the abstract quality of force but a set relationship in the individual between the different types of force that make up the individual: what one calls a type."

The master type has a direct relationship with active force. The master judges the world on the basis of his own image and reduces reality to his idea of himself: I am good, beautiful, powerful, noble, and elected. His judgment is the only active, original positive judgment.

The slave type has a different relationship to force. The plebeian's judgment reverses the master's judgment. It is negative and driven mainly by a "reactive force": the master is strong and evil; I am weak and I am therefore good.

The difference between the master type and the slave type enables Deleuze to illustrate in Nietzsche's work the dissymmetry between the will to power and ressentiment. But the comparison between "active forces" and "reactive forces" betrays Deleuze's propositions because it indirectly reveals to the reader the presence of precise analogies and symmetries between ressentiment and the will to power, a precise common matrix in the notion of "force."

In the one case, this is the "force" of noble and autonomous people. In the other case, it is the "force" of plebeian and heteronomous people. In both cases, it is the vitalist and energetic force of the will to power that is fully expressed in the noble and autonomous human being, whereas it quickly turns into ressentiment when it animates the typology of the weak human being. Deleuze's reading shows that Nietzsche adopts a theoretical model rooted in a sole basic explanatory principle: the notion of "force." The distinctive features of ressentiment, from the morality of the slaves to their unassuaged desire for revenge, share the theoretical matrix that also explains the morals of the nobles, of the strong people. The creative and destructive force of the will to power, force, that in the powerful human being flows free and vital; in the powerless human being does not recognize itself and hides behind a higher principle of love and justice. It takes on the anthropological forms of the negative and weakened reaction that is Christianity.

Deleuze shows that in Nietzsche's work the concept of force is identified with the concept of the will to power. A human being's will to power, according to Nietzsche, is measured by the basis of his capacity for self-determination, his ability to be autonomous and free from conditioning by others. The degree of autonomy of an individual in affirming him- or herself coincides with the deployment of his or her force: it will be active in the prototype of the noble human being and reactive and weakened in the prototype of the weak human being. A vicious circle is thus created, a double knot between being full of ressentiment and the will to power: full of ressentiment because one is not capable of affirming oneself, yet incapable of affirming oneself because one is full of ressentiment.

According to Nietzsche, Christ's message has sanctioned the affirmation of powerless people because the message of the Gospels leads people to admire not so much heroes or wise people as common individuals who respected, understood, and loved others and who because of that have sacrificed their desire for glory, social success, or intellectual prowess. For Nietzsche, the expansion of the secularized principles of Christianity in the modern age, of the love of one's neighbor, of solidarity, of compassion, of the principles of equality and equal dignity for all people, is a sign of a deep crisis in the will to power, which has sickened and weakened, taking on the destructive form of ressentiment.

2
Bourgeois Philanthropy

Perhaps she [Mlle. Vinteuil] would not have thought of wickedness as a state so rare, so abnormal, so exotic, one which it was so refreshing to visit, had she been able to distinguish in herself, as in all her fellow-men and women, that indifference to the sufferings which they cause which, whatever names else be given it, is the one true, terrible and lasting form of Cruelty.

—Marcel Proust, *Remembrance of Things Past*

Nietzsche's anthropological and genealogical polemic that places the ressentiment of the weak against the powerful at the origin of Christian love has been the object of numerous, often heated, debates. One of its most thorough and analytical critiques is that of Max Scheler.

In *Ressentiment im Aufbau der Moralen*, published in 1912 (translated into English as simply *Ressentiment*), Scheler explicitly undertook to prove that the thesis set out by Nietzsche in *The Genealogy of Morals* is profoundly mistaken and rests on a theoretical error. Although Nietzsche is credited with defining ressentiment in scientific terms and providing a deep analysis that deserves the highest consideration, for Scheler the Nietzschean explanation is at the end of the day "completely *false*."

According to Scheler, ressentiment did not give rise to Christianity by any means. As noted by Coser in his introduction to the translation, Scheler recognizes that "if we look at European history, we are struck by the enormous effectiveness of ressentiment in the formation of Moralities, but he distances himself from Nietzsche's opinion on ressentiment's participation in the construction of Christian morality, sustaining that 'We believe that the Christian values can very easily be perverted into *ressentiment* values and have often been thus conceived. But the core of Christian ethics has not grown on the soil of *ressentiment*.'"[1]

The Judeo-Christian tradition, according to Scheler, expresses noble love toward others that ascends toward the sublime, toward God, and not toward the flattening of values, which is the tendency of ressentiment. Christian love is the "highest" expression of human values, where love for one's neighbor is already per se a valid and vital state of Mine. Christian love is fullness and vigorous active strength, which is not fueled, as sustained by Nietzsche, by the incapacity of the individual to self-affirm.

By contrast, the destructive soil of ressentiment is instead fertile ground for the roots of Modern bourgeois morality,[2] as that of the altruistic sociology of Auguste Comte, of the political economy of Adam Smith and Ricardo, or of the democratic utilitarianism of Bentham. This is where the Nietzschean misunderstanding lies. According to Scheler, Nietzsche confuses Christian love with bourgeois morality.

The perversion of values is not the fruit of Jewish ressentiment disguised as Christian love but the most typical expression of Modern bourgeois philanthropy.

The rebellion of the slaves based on ressentiment, according to Scheler, represents the concretization of a real structure through which to interpret the world, a weltanschauung.

This conception of the world has three distinctive principles: first "democratisms," second, the priority of that which is useful over that which is vital, and third the negation of the principle of solidarity.[3] All three have in common the intrinsic incapacity of people imbued with ressentiment to attain authentic judgment, that is, independently of the conditioning of others, of the hierarchy of life values.

"Democratisms" are expressions of the modern aspiration to equality: "But the modern doctrine of equality . . . is obviously an achievement of *ressentiment*. The postulate of equality . . . seems harmless, but who does not detect behind it the desire to degrade the superior persons, those who represent a higher value, to the level of the low?"[4]

According to Scheler, even affirming the principle of the useful at the cost of vital values is a way of Canceling any hierarchy of values. If every human relationship were reduced to its utility, to a mere economic or practical relationship, the different human values that are vital to this unique dimension would be flattened and the attitude of those who call for the lowering of "those who are worth more to the lowest levels" would be legitimated.

In the same way, negating the bond of solidarity between oneself and one's neighbor is a way of legitimating this desire to lower those who are above. When people no longer recognize a deep vital link between one another, it is easier for them to belittle the vital role of people of exalted and noble spirit.

Scheler credits Nietzsche with having translated the nature of resentment into scientific terms and with having shown the efficacy of this emotional condition in building morals. This remark earned Scheler the sobriquet "the Catholic Nietzsche." But at the same time Scheler takes Nietzsche severely to task for confusing the fullness of Christian love with the typical powerlessness of ressentiment, for not recognizing in Christian love the greatest expression of the noble human being.

The Phenomenology of Ressentiment

Scheler's critique of Nietzsche's conclusions therefore rests on a very precise judgment: Nietzsche confused the nobility of Christianity with the mediocrity of bourgeois morality. However, although the Schelerian thesis distances itself from the Nietzschean analysis, it nonetheless constitutes a consistent and in-depth application of the theoretical model proposed by Nietzsche.

Scheler, in his critique of *The Genealogy of Morals*, adopts a strategy that moves in two directions. On the one hand, he refuses to apply the Nietzschean model to Christianity to explain the origin of the love on which Christianity is based. On the other hand, when he has to describe the phenomenology of ressentiment in the modern world, he recognizes the intrinsic validity of the Nietzschean model of ressentiment.[5]

Scheler proposes a sociological analysis of ressentiment understood as a phenomenology of this "*self-poisoning of the mind.*"[6]

Ressentiment is considered to be a form of psychological intoxication because it implies a desire for revenge that remains unassuaged for a long period of time: it is considered to be an emotional state that is typical of the average bourgeois who cannot help comparing himself with others in a continuous "competitive frenzy" and is also doomed to come off worse in this comparison.

The typical features of ressentiment reflect a precise psychological dynamic: the emotion is relived as a "lasting mental attitude," "a going back to the emotion with feeling, a re-feeling," and is a "movement of hostility," a "reactive impulse."[7]

The formal structure of the psychological dynamic of ressentiment is always the same. Scheler writes: "The formal structure of *ressentiment* expression is always the same: A is affirmed, valued, and praised not for its own intrinsic quality, but with the un-verbalized intention of denying, devaluating, and denigrating B."[8]

According to Scheler, the origin of ressentiment is linked to a particular attitude, to the way of Comparing oneself and others. As for Nietzsche, two different types of human beings exist, who are distinguished by different and opposite methods of Making this comparison: people who judge themselves and the hierarchy of values *before* the comparison with the other and those who make the same judgment *during* the comparison. The former are defined by Scheler as "noble" people and correspond to Nietzsche's active type; the latter people correspond to Nietzsche's reactive type and are defined as "common."

Noble human beings, unlike the "common," refer originally to themselves and to their own nature as they perceive it in reality. When comparing themselves with the other, they are serene because they are aware of their own internal qualities. They acknowledge that the other can be superior in some respects, but the comparison does not challenge their self-esteem. Noble human beings do not refuse to compare themselves with others but experience the value of their own person *prior* to any comparison with the other: "The 'noble human being' has a completely naive and non-reflective awareness of his own value and of his fullness of being, an obscure conviction which enriches every conscious moment of his existence, as if he were autonomously rooted in the universe."[9]

On the other hand, "common human beings" establish a scale of values only by comparison with others and through this comparison: they "measure" their own value only by comparing themselves with others. In this sense, the "common human being" is conscious of values (and also of their own value) only at the "moment" of Comparison.

According to Scheler, it is on the basis of the attitude typical of the "common human being" that the two subtypes are to be recognized, according as to whether the feature of the other taken to measure oneself is strength or weakness. The phenomenology of ressentiment corresponds to the subtype associated with weakness.

The emotional condition of ressentiment is, according to Scheler, closely linked to the "common" type of human being; accordingly, all the different psychological types of ressentiment-filled persons whom he describes (the woman, the priest, the old man, the mother-in-law) have a precise feature in common: their weakness, their powerlessness.

A human being's powerlessness is measured by (inversely proportional to) his or her ability to give free rein to emotions. "Revenge, envy, the impulse to detract, spite, *Schadenfreude*, and malice lead to *ressentiment* only if there occurs neither a moral self-conquest . . . nor an act or some other adequate expression of emotion . . . and if this restraint is caused by a pronounced awareness of impotence."[10]

The basic feature of Scheler's model of ressentiment is thus, as is also the case for Nietzsche, powerlessness, the inability to rise to the challenges of a comparison with the other, a powerlessness that condemns common human beings to an inevitable defeat whenever they compare themselves with the other.

A human being full of ressentiment imagines him- or herself inferior, a loser, and this psychological poisoning leads him or her to desire revenge in order to be able withstand comparison with the other. This desire for revenge leads to a *misrepresentation* of values maneuvered by resentment: this is visible, for example, in the case of a human being who belittles the values of others who oppress him or her, because, according to the formal structure that we have seen previously, he or she feels unable to embrace that positive character, precisely because of the psychological dynamic of ressentiment, where praise of A aims to belittle B.

The phenomenological analysis of ressentiment proposed by Scheler takes over the following features of Nietzsche's basic model: the purely reactive nature of ressentiment, belonging to a weak type of human being, the subversion of values (regardless of the fact that the reference values for the two authors are completely different). Further, Scheler elaborates the Nietzschean model, analytically developing it and emphasizing in particular two elements: the expression of ressentiment and the desire to measure oneself with the other.

The expressivity of gestures and grimaces that characterizes the interior obsession of ressentiment, according to Scheler, is represented by an insignificant, unexpected, and malevolent smile. "How often does *ressentiment* betray itself by a smile, a seemingly meaningless gesture, or a passing remark, in the midst of expressions of friendship and sympathy! When a malicious act or remark, apparently unfounded, is suddenly inserted into amicable or even loving behavior, which can have lasted for months, we distinctly feel that a deeper layer of life breaks through the friendly surface."[11]

This typical expression of ressentiment arises from a deep vital layer of Common human beings who harbor ressentiment because they feel the need to measure themselves through other people. Without this need, they would not expose themselves to the possibility of perceiving themselves to be a loser. On the other hand, the noble human being does not feel this need to compare him- or herself and for this reason does not harbor desires for revenge.

Scheler describes a phenomenology of ressentiment that is very similar to what we find in Nietzsche's study. Nevertheless, it would be an error to consider Scheler's model to be a mere repetition of the Nietzschean model. Compared with the latter, Scheler's phenomenology of ressentiment places greater emphasis on the relational dimension. The mutual comparison, the need for people to measure themselves with one another, plays an important explicative role in Scheler's analysis. Scheler senses the crucial role of relationships in the dynamic of ressentiment, although he is unable to fully develop this intuition because he remains too influenced by the individualistic approach of Nietzsche.

The relational aspect of the comparison with the other will be taken up again by him, in particular in the major work *Wesen und Formen der Sympathie* (1922).[12] Scheler was the first to emphasize the centrality of the relational and dynamic aspect of human relationships in general, using the concept of *Einfühlung,* which is generally translated into English by "empathy" (a term that has philological difficulties that are still the subject of Controversy). Empathy is, according to Scheler, an original human state that indicates an immediate perception of the other. *Einfühlung* enables human beings to experience sympathy, which according to Scheler is a basic human emotion. Sympathy is one of the highest expressions of the understanding of otherness and enables us to establish reciprocal communion that, in turn, enables us to experience and reexperience the feelings of the other. The themes of the relationship with the other and of the interaction between people are at the center of Scheler's ideas of "human being" and "spirit." According to Scheler, we need to overcome the conception of the "psyche" as something that is individually isolated, belonging to each human being in an absolutely precise and ineffable manner. For Scheler, the individual human being lives first in the world of the others and in the world of the community rather than in himself.

Scheler's awareness of the relational aspects of human relations is already present in his book *Ressentiment*, but his analysis remains mainly anchored in an individualistic and vitalist epistemological approach: ressentiment is born and is cultivated essentially as a vital impulse that gives rise to feelings of hostility that were long buried or violently repressed inside the individual.[13]

The vital individualistic dimension of ressentiment is not explicitly stated by Scheler, but we can appreciate the intrinsic logic therein on the basis of a simple syllogism: If it is true that the desire to compare oneself is the typical manifestation of "common" human beings, of their inability to perform an autonomous evaluation of themselves and of their vital values; if it is true that noble human beings, by contrast, do not base their judgment of either themselves or their values on the judgment of others, then it is the idea of Measuring oneself with others that indirectly reveals the nonauthenticity of the type of individual who needs the dimension of the comparison. Measuring oneself with the other is typical of an individual who feels ressentiment.

The essentially negative and individualist connotation of Comparison with the other emphasizes further our original hypothesis that Scheler's phenomenology of ressentiment constitutes a thorough and consistent development of the Nietzschean model.

Scheler uses the Nietzschean model against Nietzsche. He uses *The Genealogy of Morals* to come to the conclusion that ressentiment underlies the modern ethos (modern philanthropy, democratism, and bourgeois morality) and to rebut the Nietzschean thesis that the Christian is ipso facto a human being of ressentiment. On the one hand, the meaning of being a person of ressentiment is distinguished from the meaning of being a Christian, while the two had been identified before. On the other hand, the explanatory efficacy of the Nietzschean model is strengthened.[14]

Scheler's arguments at the theoretical level greatly contributed to consolidating the individualist and vital notion of ressentiment and to reinforcing the purely negative connotations that, as we have seen, distinguish this emotional condition and its dependence on comparison with others.

Paradoxically, through the Schelerian analysis Nietzsche's theoretical model appears to have foundations that are more solid than its conclusions. The problem thus arises of better understanding what the solid foundations are on which rests the image of ressentiment proposed in *The Genealogy of Morals*, an image that is subsequently elaborated in Scheler's study using more sophisticated instruments, on the basis of the elements that mark the person of ressentiment in modern and contemporary society. In order to answer this question, we must shift our attention to an epistemological plane; we must, in a sense, take a step backward.

3
The Surprise Box of Ressentiment

> It obliges the artist not to keep himself apart; it
> subjects him to the most humble and the most
> universal truth. And often he who has chosen
> the fate of the artist because he felt himself to be
> different soon realizes that he can maintain neither
> his art nor his difference unless he admits that he is
> like the others.
>
> —Albert Camus, Banquet Speech

At the epistemological level, a comparative reading of *The Genealogy of Morals* and *Ressentiment* shows that both works consider ressentiment and the people who feel it the same way. There are prejudices regarding ressentiment that are to a certain extent common to both authors. That is what we now need to examine.

An Explosive and Deflagrating Force

If Scheler and Nietzsche answer the question "What morality is based on ressentiment?" in diametrically opposite ways, the two authors seem to align themselves on schematic and mechanistic determinism in response to the question "What is the link between ressentiment and the modern ethos?"

Both philosophers assume that ressentiment has a force that is capable of transforming the social order, of generating a moral order. Ressentiment is able to affect social action unequivocally and in one direction only, because it has a force that is ready to explode after long being buried in the nooks and crannies of the psyche of mediocre individuals; it leads Scheler's "powerless common human being" or Nietzsche's "slave" to overthrow authentic morality and social hierarchies.

The idea that ressentiment is an explosive force is clearly shown in Deleuze's original underlining of Nietzsche's philosophical terminology. By emphasizing the importance of the Nietzschean term "force," the French writer further highlights also the vitalist and generative dimension of ressentiment as a weakened manifestation of the will to power in the modern age.

In this manner, Deleuze highlights the fact that for Nietzsche ressentiment is an emotion that by virtue of its energetic and vital value generates morals and, by virtue of its "force," determines social action, subordinating to itself the behavior of mediocre individuals. In other words, ressentiment directly transforms the social order and morals by its own force.

Scheler's approach shares the same implicit assumptions as Nietzsche, because he does not question the idea according to which ressentiment could be the emotional foundation on which is built a moral order, but only criticizes the conclusion that ressentiment is the emotional condition that, in particular, is the foundation of Christian morality.

For both philosophers, ressentiment is a "force" that is similar to a type of instinct, or energetic drive toward historical and social change.

Essentialist and Individualist Psychology

According to Theodor W. Adorno,[1] Nietzsche showed the danger underlying the *thought of depth* that does not limit itself to the surface and attributes a form of substantial nature to what is below the surface, to what is hidden. This thought is not content with the facade and is obsessed by a temptation to exalt a hidden essence, which it considers to be the true content behind the facade, as if in the depths there existed certain "actualities."

According to the founder of the Frankfurt School, the author of *The Genealogy of Morals* through his work revealed the "irrational forests," the forests of the interior, the underground places, where the essences and these presumed actualities take shape. It is with this lesson of Adorno's in mind that Jürgen Habermas defined Nietzsche as a "cultural critic" who dismantled social and psychological, moral and metaphysical hypocrisies.[2]

Nietzsche's greatness certainly lies in having shown that there is no such thing as an intrinsic value, a "per se of things" nor even an essence hidden behind the facade of human affairs. However, the Nietzschean image of ressentiment seems to betray an essentialist nature that is similar to those that inhabit the "irrational forests" that the German philosopher has tried to dismantle. Has Nietzsche, the critic of the last foundation of historical and metaphysical truths, paradoxically proposed an essentialist model of ressentiment?

In my opinion, the answer to this question must be sought in Nietzsche's implicit theoretical assumption not only that weaker and more fragile people can hide rancor and hate, but also, as we have seen, that there is a coincidence between weak individuals and individuals full of ressentiment, as if weakness were an essential quality of a certain type of individuals and of emotions. Nietzsche goes as far as to maintain that ressentiment belongs only to certain categories of weak individuals because this emotion is rooted in their incomplete will to power.

The fragile type of individual is bound to be full of ressentiment because his will to power is weak, without the power of self-determination. Such individuals are not self-sufficient; they depend on the other (the "noble"); that is, their will is incomplete, and because of that they are incapable of avenging themselves and of responding openly to offenses from others. By contrast, individuals of the strong type cannot be full of ressentiment because their will to power is strong, autonomous, independent of the other (the "slave"); that is, their will is complete, therefore free and impermeable to offense.

This deep (essential) link between a certain type of individual and his or her power is also emphasized by Scheler when he conducts his own analysis of how different subtypes of people react to the comparison with others: depending on how powerful a human being is, this comparison will lead either to ambitious self-assertion or to a "resentful" misplacement of values. Scheler writes: "Then the oppressive sense of inferiority, which always goes with the 'common' attitude cannot lead to active behavior. Yet the painful tension demands relief. This is afforded by the specific *value delusion of ressentiment*."[3]

Ressentiment is the "common" human being's solution to the tension produced by the oppressive awareness of one's own inferiority. As we have seen, "common" human beings live immersed in a competitive frenzy, which leads them incessantly into the error of comparing themselves with others to have the confirmation, or the nonconfirmation, of their own values and of the authenticity of their hierarchy of values. "Noble" human beings, on the contrary, live in the fullness of their lives, sure of themselves and of their value, as occurs with the authentic Christian, who ignores the instrumental dimension of life because they trust in a deeper (essential) value of life.

This concept of ressentiment as an emotive condition proceeding from the weakness of a certain category of individuals betrays an essentialist image of ressentiment. Nietzsche and Scheler locate ressentiment in the lack of *power* of weak individuals and thus contribute to the construction of a very precise image of this emotion. It is as if it could belong only to a certain anthropological and social type of individual, as if it were an essence that emerges from the incomplete power of those individuals and not from their interaction with others.

Both philosophers certainly showed great perspicacity in recognizing the crucial role that ressentiment plays in human relationships in the modern era, but also reduced it to an emotional event that coincides only with the mediocrity of a certain category of individuals. It is attributed to the insufficient force of certain types of individual persons. This neglects the possibility that ressentiment is an emotion that arises from communicative interactions and that can affect the (social and natural) condition of any human being, not only weak and fragile individuals, but also of "elevated" or "noble" people without there being any necessary link between the power of an individual and his or her nursing a grudge.

The Negative Image of Human Fragility

The reader of *The Genealogy of Morals* and of *Ressentiment* finds in both books a profoundly negative image of human frailty in modern society.

The words used by Scheler to explain the ressentiment

of bourgeois morals are often harsher and "harder on the ears" than those used by Nietzsche to describe the Christian lowness of "slave morals." It seems that their fixation on ressentiment reveals contempt for modern human beings, who have forgotten the desire for glory (Nietzsche) or the authentic search for the values of life (Scheler), and who are content to live in a warm interior and with a full belly.

In Nietzsche, the type of human being that more than any other embodies this negative connotation is the ascetic priest. Such a person, according to Nietzsche, embodies the most decadent expression of modern ressentiment: it is the spirit of the slave who searches for small pleasures in organizing his flock, deeply bored with himself and falsely satisfied with the prosperity of the community of believers. Nietzsche writes: "Here an attempt is being made to use one's power to block up the sources of that power. Here one directs one's gaze, with a green malice, against one's inherent physiological health, particularly against its means of expression—beauty and joy."[4]

Every manifestation of human fragility is negative, because it constitutes the motor of modern decadence. The human beings of modern society are sick human beings. They are "physiologically impaired and worm-eaten"; they are envious of the happiness of noble human beings and want to react by using their sickness as a crutch. Incapable of "justifying, explaining and affirming themselves," they seek their affirmation by negating life. They are people without objectives, without ideals, fragile and on the edge of neuroses: they are vulnerable to mediocre feelings and to abnormal ressentiment.

In the wake of this configuration of ideas and values, Nietzsche does not limit himself to describing an emotion and explaining its historical and social genesis. He goes further, to outline human fragility as the most negative vital form of the modern age. He defines it as the modern age's ill par excellence.

This unequivocally negative connotation of human fragility is taken up by Scheler when he describes modern humanitarianism. Although for him the emblem of modern decadence admittedly does not coincide with the ascetic, but with the philanthropist, this second type of common human being remains sordid and sick. Scheler does not hesitate to condemn severely the misplacement of values operated by the bourgeois: "But it is not sufficiently clear that this generally acknowledged fact is due to a fundamental *subversion of values. Its source is* ressentiment, the victory of the value judgments of those who are vitally inferior, of the lowest, the pariahs of the human race!"[5]

The spread of the "common" people is the linchpin of the twilight of modernity and coincides with the ascent and decline of the bourgeois world: the value of what has been "earned with one's own work," instead of social solidarity, the value of profit that dethrones the value of life in general— these, as we have seen, are symbols of the misplacement of values by persons of ressentiment. According to Norberto Bobbio,[6] in Scheler the concept of the bourgeois human being acts as a type of container in which to enclose all of the world's evils and from which he extracts them at will; it is, in other words, a "box full of surprises."

For both philosophers, the evil of ressentiment lies in its ability to pervert the vital principles of existence, to transform fragility into a harmfully creative source. According to Nietzsche, this capacity is manifested in the inversion of the natural relationship between life and the will to power: in this case it is the will to power that moves against life, weakness that sets itself up as a unit of measurement of human resources. According to Scheler, this capacity is found in the reversal of the authentic hierarchy of values in the "subversion of the value judgment," in which constant comparisons with the other progressively takes the place of the authentic search for values.

Nietzsche and Scheler condemn human fragility on the basis of an implicit theoretical construct. First, both postulate a priori a value that is positive per se: the vital for Nietzsche, the authentic for Scheler. Subsequently, on the basis of this postulation both delineate a dichotomy of irreconcilable opposites, between the positive and the negative, between the complete and the incomplete, the strong and the weak.

The epistemological construct of the two authors examined here, that is, the tendency to simplify reality according to a dualist scheme, as we shall see in greater detail in subsequent sections, can be considered to be one of the most widespread and oldest ways of interpreting human events. In his last work, *I sommersi e i salvati* (*The Drowned and the Saved*), Primo Levi, writer and survivor of the genocide at Auschwitz, reflects on his experiences in the extermination camp. He intentionally describes with epistemological lucidity the dualistic tendency that eliminates all *gray areas* in human affairs: "The need to divide the field into 'we' and 'they' is so strong that this pattern, this bipartition–friend/enemy–prevails over all others. Popular history . . . is influenced by this Manichean tendency, which shuns half-tints and complexities: it is prone to reduce the river of human occurrences to conflicts, and the conflicts to duels—we and they, Athenians and Spartans, Romans and Carthaginians."[7] Levi asks us not to simplify and not to transform the boundaries between me and the other into easy separations: the limit between me and the other is never completely clear in interpersonal relations, in which we are always interlinked.

It is in this dualist manner that our two authors identify fragility only in those who lack vitality or only in those who lack authenticity, as if it were an inextirpable evil rooted in certain individuals defined negatively a priori. The conclusion of the two authors is a bitter tautology: individuals are full of ressentiment because they are fragile, and individuals are fragile because they are full of ressentiment.

The Modern Banquet

The analysis of the Nietzsche's and Scheler's models shows that their evaluation of ressentiment rests on common prejudices. The different distinctive features that constitute the "ressentiment object" (the desire for revenge, the type of individuals, the subversion of values, the competitive frenzy) for both authors should be viewed as a wider framework relative to the particular manners of conceiving this particular object adopted by Nietzsche and Scheler. The distinctive features of this way of conceiving ressentiment are the energetic idea of generative force able to produce a form of morals and to change the social order; the essentialist and individualistic psychology of this emotion, according to which the essence of ressentiment coincides with the mediocrity of some individuals taken individually; and the condemnation of common and fragile people destined by "nature" to live this emotional condition.

Nietzsche outlined an image of ressentiment based on an idea of emotions as individual private phenomena. In this context, emotions subject to the influence of others constitute a sign of immaturity and weakness. To some extent, Scheler sensed that this individualistic psychology itself arises from the logic that leads to ressentiment. He nevertheless was unable to fully develop this intuition because he remained too influenced by the Nietzschean model.

These two masters of Western thought nevertheless had the merit of placing ressentiment at the center of modern social and cultural transformations. Their diagnosis of modern society supposes that in the modern age everyone inevitably has, directly or indirectly, to address this evil, even the best people: "slaves" because they are destined to harbor a desire for revenge that remains unassuaged; "masters" because they are exposed to the poison of servile people; "ascetics" because they are driven by a petty desire for revenge when they profess love for their neighbor; "bourgeois" because they are corrupted by democratism and by the false altruism of modernity. All are full of ressentiment like the fox in Aesop's famous fable fascinated by the mass of hanging grapes that he cannot reach.

From the two authors we examined we obtain a clear and lucid image of modern ressentiment, the lesson of which is that ressentiment (and ressentiment theory) is too keen on criticizing the imperfections of others to be able to recognize these shortcomings in itself. This image constitutes a large fresco of the modern age, where a rich banquet is painted. There are many guests, each with his own biography, and some sit opposite one another: the "slaves" and the "masters," on one side, and the ascetics, "bourgeois," and "common people" on the other. The banquet has been prepared carefully. On the table there are precious objects: Judeo-Christian morals, democracy, and progress. The guests are cozy with full bellies, but they are not happy; they accuse one another in a round of retaliation where each plays at being an obstacle for the other. They are in ferment. The rich banquet is a box of surprises that hides a trick: the only dish served is sour grapes.

4
The Last of the Scapegoats

It is a piece of received wisdom that in every group, there exists a predetermined victim: one who carries pain, whom everyone mocks, on whom they heap stupid and malevolent rumours, and with mysterious agreement everyone unloads their negative feelings and their desire to harm.

—Primo Levi, *The Truce*

The genesis of ressentiment interrogates the *foundation* of human coexistence, by emphasizing the close and vital relationship between the affective human condition and the genesis of the political and institutional order.

There is no easy answer to such a question, but we shall attempt to answer with the help of the mimetic theory of René

Girard[1] and its subsequent theoretical elaborations.[2] Girard gives an intriguing answer to our question that is equally difficult for common understanding to grasp. The answer lies in the figure of the scapegoat, defined as the linchpin on which the entire hominization process rests. Girard's theory revisits in a radical way the Freudian image of a founding murder. Girard's idea seems to be a "countermelody" to Freud's *Totem und Tabu* (*Totem and Taboo*).[3] The difference between the anthropological hypotheses of the two authors should, however, be emphasized: for Freud, the founding murder refers to the murder of the father, whereas for Girard it is a question, as we shall see below, of the sacrifice of any innocent victim designated by a victimary process.

Man, language, culture, customs, symbols, and rules have, according to Girard, a close relation with violence and a process of violent exclusion: "the violence directed against the surrogate victim might well be radically generative in that, by putting an end to the vicious and destructive cycle of violence, it simultaneously initiates another and constructive cycle, that of the sacrificial rite—which protects the community from that same violence and allows culture to flourish."[4]

In the history of humanity, the scapegoat, or more generally the victimary process, is for Girard the starting point of civilization. It is also the point where violence and the sacred are joined. In Girard, as Paul Valadier remarked, "The religious coincides with the hominisation of man."[5] Girard's theory of the scapegoat can be compared with Durkheim's anthropological theory of the social. The main similarity between the two positions on the origin of the first organized forms of the social relates to the false transcendence of the sacred. The sacred is for both of them a lie (according to Durkheim the "totem" is an illusory representation of "society") that all members of the community respect and obey until it is unmasked. Nevertheless, a comparison between Girard's hypothesis and Durkheim's shows that it would be a mistake to define Girard's thesis as "Durkheimian": in Durkheim's social anthropology certain categories are absent that are of primary importance in the mimetic theory; the victimary process, the "scapegoat," and, above all, the insurmountable difference between archaic religions and Christian religion.

The "scapegoat" is an innocent victim who draws on himself the violence of a community torn internally by the heightening of rivalries and the spread of mutual hatred. To better understand this concept, we must examine Girard's usage of the term "scapegoat." Girard does not use the concept in ritual sense, but to describe the result of a spontaneous psychosocial process: the "scapegoat" is someone who is blamed for the mistakes or sins of others. Girard uses the concept of "scapegoat" to highlight the unconscious psychosocial nature of this solution of social crisis.

The community is divided by multiple opposing desires for revenge and would collapse if it did not resort to the corrective measure provided by the "victimage mechanism," which acts as a restraint on an otherwise inevitable process of self-destruction.

Through the victimary process, the community institutes an unbridgeable gap between itself and the victim. The original killing of the victim achieves a catharsis of the community. The persecutors, previously divided by reciprocal hatred, are united at the moment of killing by their common aversion for the victim. On the ashes of the "scapegoat" a new order is thus created: the survivors are then caught up in a narrative that transforms the execrated victim into a hero who is a savior that is able to restore order and peace. This empty space between the victim and the survivors is suddenly taken up by the sacred.

The metamorphosis of the scapegoat into a sacred being is for Girard the creation of the "social transcendence": "If this victim can extend his benefits beyond death to those who have killed him, he must either be resuscitated or was not truly dead. The causality of the scapegoat is imposed with such force that even death cannot prevent it. In order not to renounce the victim's causality, he is brought back to life and immortalized, temporarily, and what we call the transcendent and supernatural are invented for that purpose."[6]

Girard's thorough analysis of the mythical texts belonging to the Western, Greek, African, and Central American tradition has shown that the myths and the rites, that is, the first forms of sacred expression, are the result of a process of symbolization of this original violence.[7] The term *ritual* here refers to one of the first stages that make up the slow process of increasingly refined repetition for the founding murder. According to Girard, it is possible to conceive the victimary process in initially crude and elementary forms that are very difficult to represent. The concept of symbolization is defined by Girard as a process of rationalization and misunderstanding of violence that uses cut-and-dried contrasts and a dualistic scheme (good versus evil, us against them, etc.) based on the illusion of a difference that is imagined to be absolute and total.[8]

This process of symbolic reworking is, according to Girard, the basis of all human cultural expressions. In archaic societies men tried to prevent the spreading of the insidious poisons of mutual hatred and the destructive effects of mutual violence and of revenge[9] with myths and rites that became increasingly refined on the symbolic level. Through ritual practices, men have tried to perfect prohibitions, and through myths they have tried to consolidate the cultural sacrificial order.

For this reason, archaic societies long remained trapped in the vicious circle of violence and the sacred: men remedied the spread of reciprocal violence unconsciously, using social standards and institutions (myths, rites, sacrifices, and prohibitions) that were in turn sustained by the ordering power of violence (scapegoat, victimary process).

Girard has undoubtedly shown in his different works the tragically generative and ordering dimension of the relationship between the sacred and violence. The social order, the pacific coexistence between men, according to Girard, is rooted in the sacrificial system: every human society is built around its scapegoats and is consolidated by shared myths, cyclically proposing ever more sophisticated forms of mythical narrative, of persecution, and of exclusion.

We now need to understand the story of the scapegoat and of its intimate relationship with human, collective, and individual affairs.

The Christian Revelation of Ritual Violence

In Girard's view, at a certain point in the history of human civilization the pacifying "mechanisms" of exclusion and of persecuting violence gradually started to lose their efficacy. According to Girard, it was Christian revelation that triggered this unstoppable erosion of the sacred order of myths and rites: "The Bible enables us to decipher what we have learnt to identify in persecutors' representations of persecution. . . . The Gospels . . . center around the Passion of Christ, the same drama that is found in all the world's mythologies. . . . Thus the same drama is needed to give birth to the only text that can bring an end to all of mythology."[10]

Using a thorough exegesis of the Old and New Testaments, Girard shows that the figure of Jesus Christ is the protagonist of a radical transformation of the victimary process, that is, of the relationship between mythology, ritual practices, and violence.

Christ's revelation laid bare men's tragic inability to reconcile themselves without exclusions, without sacrifices, without killing, and above all *without scapegoats*. Christ reveals that it is we men, and not the god-heroes of the mythical world, who are the sole creators of our violence. Christian revelation, according to Girard, denounced the violence of the god-heroes and disapproved of murder. For the first time, sacrifice was in a radical way unable to create peace anew inside the community.

Christ, like the other expiatory victims who preceded him, was doomed to be the scapegoat of a community that was on the verge of destroying itself. But Christ, instead of reconciling the persecutors to one another, upset them, confronting them with the blinding light of a revelation that placed in their hands the effects of their actions.

Christ stood up to the accusations, declared his innocence, and moreover did not yield to the desire for revenge. Using parables about the innocence of the excluded, he laid bare the bloody link between the violence of the community and the sacred world of the god-heroes. In this way he prevented his persecutors from completing the cycle of persecution, from effectively completing the process of sacrificing the scapegoat. This aspect of Christ's Passion marks the main difference between mythology and the Christian tradition. The figure of Christ, unlike the other innocent victims of the pagan tradition, revealed the persecutory nature of violence.

The revelation of the Gospels means that men witness the progressive loss of the ordering power of their sacrificial violence. In pre-Christian societies, the escalation of violence and revenge was controlled by the sacred: ritual and religious prohibitions constituted an effective brake on the spreading of violence. However, according to Girard, following the

Christian revelation those purifying and ordering forms progressively lost their sacred aura. According to Gianni Vattimo, Girard's theory shows that the process of secularization in the modern age is the true implementation of Christianity.[11] The secularization of the strong structures of myth and metaphysics is an opportunity offered to modern man for a new and peaceful coexistence. Nevertheless, as Vattimo wrote, Girard thinks that this interpretation of his opinions is too "optimistic." For Girard, secularization is certainly not devoid of tragic effects.

The breakdown of the regenerative source of the sacred that rested on the persecution of scapegoats undermined the prohibitions that were consecrated in rites and were necessary for restraining competition and violence between men.

After Christ, new horizons open up to men: they can become reconciled to one another without exclusions and without scapegoats. This new and important opportunity does not, however, eliminate the risk that men will still resort to violence. They are freed from the burdens of violence and of the pagan sacred, but this liberation is not devoid of tragic aspects. In the Christian era men in fact progressively lose all alibis for legitimizing their violence, and this loss makes resorting to "legitimate" violence ineffective for expelling "illegitimate" violence and for maintaining social order.

The revelation of the Gospels indicates the possibility of relating to one another in a new way. This opportunity has marked a profound transformation in human dealings that has modified set historical and cultural orders. Christian revelation started and still continues to supply a slow, but unstoppable process of secularization of political and institutional orders. At the same time, the decline of the ordering and pacifying power of social institutions leads men to take new decisions regarding social interaction. There is thus the possibility of achieving reconciliation without sacrificing innocent victims. The gaze of the mimetic actor is increasingly recognizable as a gaze that is reflected in the gaze of its models, who therefore become nearer and nearer.

The end of the pagan sacred gradually leads to the erosion of the social order, abandoning men to the disturbing awareness of being solely responsible for their social action. Each one discovers that he lives from birth to death in an unfathomable tragedy marked by decisions that always bring with them the possibility of conflict and collaboration, of hatred and ressentiment, and of revenge and forgiveness. The outcome of social actions no longer depends on the gods, on destiny, or on our scapegoats, but only on our own choices.

The Basic Anthropology of the Bible

Girard provides this diagnosis of our era on the basis of an interpretation of Western history as a manifestation of the hidden workings of Christian revelation, which corrodes from the inside the bases of a social and cultural order rooted in the millennia of violence of the victimary process.

This interpretation of Western civilization recognizes that men in Christian society live in a new anthropological condition. Our symbolic universe, which has been deeply marked by the crisis of traditional ritual forms, risks depriving modern man of an effective antidote to the spread of human violence. Men run the risk of abandoning themselves to competition, to rivalry and mutual hatred, without being able to resort to the ordering force of the scapegoat. In other words, they have to invent and experiment with new forms of social coexistence that have never been implemented before.

In the Christian universe, according to Girard, the risk of being defenseless against our violence increases and spreads. Christian revelation deprived men of any justification for their violence: they find that they are the sole makers of their own dark side. After Christ, no demon or false hero can take responsibility for our misdeeds; no scapegoat can stop the spread of reciprocal violence.

In order to address this new anthropological condition that gradually spreads with Christian revelation, Girard writes: "We must give up making our society and above all the Judaeo-Christian tradition, our scapegoats. . . . We must loyally, openly, practice a new freedom, a very difficult freedom."[12]

In order to illustrate the nature of violence fully, to understand how much human destiny is caught up in its own violence, according to Girard we not only have to forgo not only scapegoats, but also the very concept of the scapegoat.

A first movement in this direction is to reject certain

explanations, including many scientific explanations, of the origins of violence that seem to lay bare human violence, but actually mistake its deep causes and end up confirming and feeding it. The explanations that should be abandoned are those that refer to prior factors behind the violent behaviors, which are the object of the explanation, for example, interior psychological aspects of the individual or his or her biological nature or exterior characteristics, like the family environment, the workings of the capitalist market, or other social or religious institutions. The matrix of violence is thus sought *elsewhere* than in the concrete and immediate interplay of the human relationships that are to be explained.

For Girard, these explanations are a way of mistaking the violence that arises from our actions; they are new alibis for finding mythological justifications for our actions, as if the explanatory categories of the demons or god-heroes of Olympus were replaced by those of the market, of the family environment, of society or nature, and of the psyche.

This also applies when the explanations are accompanied by the nonviolent intention to combat the violence. Girard writes that it is typical of modern ressentiment to hide behind good and enlightened intentions: "the modern mind . . . resorts to an ideal of nonviolence . . . as a covertly violent criterion for all judgments and critical evaluations."[13]

Rising to Girard's epistemological challenge means giving up searching for the origins of violence in a single cause separated from human interactions. It means considering violence from a unique perspective: not as if it were a basis in itself, regardless of the men who practice it, but as an expression of our actions, of our relationships, and of our desires, as a form that is tragically a constituent part of reciprocal relationships between human beings.

More exactly, the violence that arises from our actions, even from the most well intentioned actions, stems for Girard from an inherent characteristic of the communicative relationships that connect human beings. Girard's reflection on the dynamics of desire refers to this relational dimension. Girard proposes to analyze desire from an unusual perspective, one that is so unusual that we can talk of a "Copernican devolution" relative to more established methods of investigating desire and its relationship with violence.[14]

According to Girard, Christ's revelation obliges us to direct our gaze to the essential aspects of human relations and to acknowledge violence as a constantly possible outcome that is intrinsic to human interactions: the desire to be like the other, or more briefly, mimesis.

The Modern Underground of Ressentiment

While not diverting our attention from the "undergrounds" of the modern world brought into light by Nietzsche, mimetic theory takes a completely different view of the undergrounds. According to Girard, Nietzsche was the first to grasp that an essential and typical aspect of modernity is that it entails an expansion of ressentiment and that this increase is a fruit of Christianity.[15]

In the history of the West, for Girard as for Nietzsche, the figure of Christ marks the epoch-making transition that radically transformed the relationship between violence and the sacred, leading to the collapse of the traditional sacred order and of the figure of the god-hero of myths and rites.

The rupture of the immediate link between the ordering power of violence and the sacred by Christian revelation generated the secularization process that characterizes modernity.

The Christian message renders ineffective sacrificial institutions that were vital for maintaining prohibitions and the social order. As these institutions became increasingly ineffective in controlling and stemming our violence, modern men risked being left with no defenses against their own violence, against reciprocal hatred and ressentiment. The weakening of the mythical-ritual order in the modern world enables ressentiment to prosper in new forms of oppression and persecution that are so powerful as to take on the form of genocide. The story of the twentieth century with its tragic expressions of hatred and violence can be seen as a terrible vindication of the Nietzschean analyses.

Nevertheless, the French thinker does not draw the same conclusions as the German philosopher. While acknowledging that Nietzsche drew attention to the drama at the heart of the secularization processes, Girard subjects to close critical examination the theoretical suppositions that support Nietzsche's analysis and in the end proposes a very different diagnosis of the relation between ressentiment and modernity. "Nietzsche sees *ressentiment* not only as Christianity's child, which is certainly true, but also as its father, which is certainly false."[16]

According to Girard,[17] Nietzsche absolutely rejected the Christian message and its secularized forms, that is, modernity, because he overlooked another constituent aspect of this revelation, namely the fact that Christ's message not only mortally wounds the pagan sacred order, but *also* offers men the opportunity of a new way of reconciling themselves, one that leaves them no excuse for the violence that they do to one another. That is precisely the reason why the Christian revelation opens up the possibility of *new ways* in which men could relate to one another.

Christian revelation has revealed the nature of violence, of the exclusion and persecution of innocent victims; it has shown humans that they have been incapable of reconciling themselves with one another and that they bear the complete responsibility for all violence. However, according to Girard, Christ also gave us the chance to recognize in our neighbor the other who is identical to us, who has the same responsibilities and incapacities, and gave us the possibility of being reconciled through a gesture of love, instead of resorting to exclusion or violence.

Girard reaches this deconstruction of the Nietzschean perspective by elaborating a thorough academic investigation of what Simone Weil defined as the "theory of man" found in the Judeo-Christian tradition of the Old and New Testaments. The rigorous theoretical model of human relations mentioned above, that of mimetic desire or the mimetic theory, guided this investigation.

In order to understand the deep meaning assigned by Girard to the relationship between ressentiment and the transformations of modern society, we must assume a mimetic and relational theoretical reading of human relationships, one that is able to summarize the new and radical image of man revealed by the Gospels.

The difference from the Nietzschean approach and outcome is clear and evident. Once one has made one's own the theoretical aspiration, which is Nietzsche's, of understanding the profound nature of the principles of equality, solidarity, and democracy that are typical of the modern era, Girard calls on us to first step back, in a sense, and to appreciate the anthropological importance of the relationship of reciprocal dependence of each one on the other. This step backward is indispensable for continuing the path of modern men, of which only the Gospels have fully indicated the need.

5
The Mimetic Nature of Our Ressentiment

Having disburdened his heart, the Inquisitor waits for some time to hear his prisoner speak in His turn. His silence weighs upon him. He has seen that his captive has been attentively listening to him all the time, with His eyes fixed penetratingly and softly on the face of his jailer, and evidently bent upon not replying to him. The old man longs to hear His voice, to hear Him reply; better words of bitterness and scorn than His silence. Suddenly He rises; slowly and silently approaching the Inquisitor, He bends towards him and softly kisses the bloodless four-score-and-ten-year-old lips. That is all the answer.

—Fyodor Dostoyevsky, *The Brothers Karamazov*

For Girard, our desire is not a private, individual matter hidden away in our inner "cubbyhole" but a work in which several people are involved, and which exists only in relation to others and thanks to them. The life of our desires is a life shared with the desires of other men, regulated by a logic that is constitutionally relational. Our desire, according to Girard, is always a desire to be like the other. The Girardian actor is a mimetic actor, pushed by a passionate admiration for the other, who in his eyes takes on the role of a mediator. The life of each of us is the story of our relationships with our models, with the persons whom we deeply desire to be and whose gestures and style we accordingly imitate. This is not a simple repetitive and passive imitation of the other, but an active imitation that is reciprocal and hence often also conflictual.

In fact, the people we most admire can also be the people we hate most, because we should like to be in their place, but we are prevented in this by their very presence. In other words, Girard suggests that admiration for our models often ends up hiding the competitive and violently antagonistic nature of our relationship to them. This human condition has in the modern age taken on very somber colors: modern man is deeply trapped in the undergrounds of rivalry, competition, envy, from which it becomes more difficult to reemerge the more we insist on hiding the relational character of life, which depends on the constitutionally mimetic nature of the emotional conditions.

In order to substantiate this intuition of Girard's we shall accordingly reconstruct the theoretical nucleus of the notion of mimesis, that, together with the notion of the scapegoat, are the explicative principles on which Girard's entire cathedral is built.

We pursue two objectives. On the one hand we shall try to outline the theoretical premises of Girard's theoretical architecture that are required to *extend* the mimetic model for interpreting ressentiment in contemporary society. At another level, we shall direct our attention to the epistemological challenge of the "mimetic" reading proposed by the Gospels, that is, the recognition of the new and radical image of man found in the Gospels.

Ressentiment and the Desire to Be Like the Other

Mimetic desire is above all a relational dynamic. Mimetic desire, desire according to the other, is thus opposed to the classic image of desire as an individual pulsation or psychic instance: desire is not a predisposition internal to the individual. It is not the product of cultural, economic, or social infrastructures. Its goal is not the possession of an object that is desirable for its economic value or for its presumed objective qualities. In other words, the generative source of desire does not lie within the single individual or outside him either, but in the relations between individuals.[1]

According to Girard, more exactly desire takes shape inside the triangular relationship between the subject, his or her model, and the object. The subject desires the object desired by the model, and the object therefore takes second place, leaving the social relationships at the front scene. The object can be a person, a symbol, a social status, or anything else; what counts is simply that it is desired by the model. The driving force of desire is the model, a model that every mimetic actor carries within himself and that deletes or blurs the boundaries between intimacy and alterity. Even with a simple gesture the model can exert a fascination that is often unconscious that invites us to imitate it.

In addition to being relational, desire is generative, in the sense that it creates and re-creates incessantly its own objects according to the type of mimetic relations that govern it. This generative connotation of Girard's idea of desire introduces a profound break with the traditional idea of imitation (such as Plato's) that is closely linked to an idea of passive repetition.

Within the sociological tradition, Gabriel Tarde had already theorized the "law of imitation"[2] defined as a universal principle, a human tendency to copy the actions of the other, which would explain the regularity of society. Nevertheless, this definition of imitation does not explain change or social conflict, because it does not fully include the generative and dynamic dimension of imitation.

The active dimension of imitation, according to Girard, is explained by the fact that reciprocal imitation is an imitation of desire: each of us imitates the desire of his or her own model and each of us, at the same time, is a model for another. This reciprocity of desire feeds rivalry and competition: in fact, two desires that imitate one another cannot but converge on a single horizon, and this inevitably leads to a risk of conflict.

This is perhaps the most difficult aspect of mimesis to accept: the idea that the people whom we most admire can suddenly turn out to be the people whom we most hate and that our models that are so admired and loved can be transformed into our worst rivals, into the source of our ressentiment. Or that in the worst of our rivals may hide a secretly admired and envied model.

From this perspective, ressentiment is a form of human relations, a form of our desire according to the other. Ressentiment is, as Girard writes, what "the imitator feels about his model when the model hinders his efforts to gain possession of the object on which both converge."[3]

The idea that imitation creates a link that is such as to generate admiration and ressentiment in equal measure, obliges us to consider the paradoxical character of desire. The condition of being according to the other is, by definition, recursive. As in Escher's *Hands Drawing Themselves*, in this condition opposite instances coexist in a double reciprocal implication: the other is a rival because he or she is a model, and a model because a rival.[4] For Girard, this idea is closely connected to Gregory Bateson's notion of double bind.[5] If the subject desires to be according to the other, the other will always possess what the subject desires: it will at the same time be the model that excites my desire and that is the obstacle to its satisfaction.

Mimesis feeds on this paradoxical structure that configures the relationship that connects mimetic actors: for mimetic desire, nothing is more desirable than what is unreachable and this is why the obstacle exerts an irresistible fascination. As we have already said, the subject desires the object because the other desires it, or possesses it. By choosing a model, the mimetic actor automatically chooses a rival, an obstacle, and this becomes a way of desiring even more intensely.

The Ambivalence of Desire

From a theoretical point of view, the mimetic condition, that of being according to the other, is not only relational, generative, and paradoxical; it is also not marked by either a negative or a positive value *in se*; it is of an intrinsically ambivalent nature.

As we have seen, reciprocal imitation generates rivalry and competition, which are both at the origin of the processes of development of human civilization and at the basis of the processes that lead to ressentiment and exclusion. Mimetic desire that feeds admiration for our models can always "change sign" and generate hatred and violence. On the other hand, hatred and violence can generate alliances, collaboration, and friendship. Mimesis is thus a relationship that can take on different social forms. In studies following the elaboration of the mimetic theory different mimetic figures have been identified and many others still need to be reconstructed. Some of these are the double, the narcissist, the scapegoat,[6] and the solipsist, the anticonformist, the minimalist.[7]

One good example of the ambivalent nature of mimetic desire is envy. Envy can be described as an extreme form of mimesis that increases progressively as the desire to possess what the other possesses becomes unattainable.[8]

For Girard, envy is not per se an evil to be eradicated. It can "change meaning." It is the driving force behind competition and can be an occasion for growth and progress. Envying somebody can be a stimulus to improving oneself, looking for a better job, changing our general situation in life.

However, envy can lead to the worst atrocities: envy can be the cause of frustration or of rivalry that is almost self-destructive. The more the mimetic actor tries to achieve his desires, the more he exposes himself to conflict with the model-rival. This conflict that tends toward a lack of differentiation, toward absolute equality with the rival, can lead to violence. Rivalry tends to make men ever closer to one another, tends to turn them all into murderers. Envy generates desires that tend with increasing intensity toward an identical and reciprocal outcome: that of crushing the rival.

This characteristic of mimetic envy, which is to make rivals more and more uniform, similar to each other, is, as an explanation of conflict, diametrically opposed to the approach that is typical of a whole line of Western thought (from Heraclitus to Marx), according to which conflict is rooted in difference. From a mimetic point of view, it is not the "fact" of religious, cultural, or ethical differences that triggers discriminatory behaviors toward the rival. Discrimination is not the result of the irreconcilable "force" of prejudices in the minds of persecutors, as many well-intentioned humanitarian perceptions would have it.

The matrix of conflict and violence is not to be found in the divergence of desires but in their untrammeled convergence, which corresponds to a rigorous scheme. What is at stake is the formation of reciprocal identity that affects interpersonal relationships and transforms both the political and institutional orders.

Even if Christian societies are also characterized by increasing awareness of mimetic dynamics and of the perverse nature of our desires, interactive processes nevertheless remain regulated by these unconscious dynamics. Mimetic actors are unable to foresee a priori what will occur in the dynamic processes of which they are part. Their identity is too connected to that of the others for mimetic actors to be able to decide singly and independently the fate of the social action in which they are engaged. The circular dimension of the mimetic phenomena that play out between individuals cannot be fully grasped consciously. The dimension of being according to the other necessarily implies unavoidable "ignorance" on the mimetic actor's part of the relational dynamics that involve him together with the other actors.

For example, a loving gesture may not always be taken as such by our interlocutor and may thus be misunderstood. The other might in fact interpret our renouncement of rivalry as a ruse to overcome him or her. The fact that one of the rivals forgoes the duel does not mean that the other one will do the same. There is no preset formula, no optimal strategy that is applicable in every context for forgoing a resumption of mimesis. In other words, the mimetic actor acts within social relations that transcend him or her, and this anthropological condition highlights the inadequacy of the human actor, his or her incompleteness. The mimetic anthropology is similar, albeit only partially, to that of Arnold Ghelen, to the "non finished being."[9] The mimetic actor is missing something and is mimetic precisely for this reason and is constantly seeking to fill, by mirroring himself in the other, an emptiness that nonetheless inevitably remains.

Ressentiment in Contemporary Society

A mimetic genealogy of ressentiment diagnoses the relationship between Christian revelation and modernity in a completely different way than do the analyses of Nietzsche and Scheler. It displaces the level of analysis concerning the other, to the link between human relationships and institutional order, showing how our destiny changes according to social relationships.

It entails a radical break with the individualist and vitalist image inherited from Nietzsche and Scheler and with their "pessimistic" reading of the close relationship between ressentiment and modern democracy. Both philosophers condemn and reject democracy absolutely, as well as the world of *rights* that dawned in the modern age, describing both as manifestations of the weakness and decadence of individuals who are unable to be autonomous, self-sufficient, and independent of others. This condemnation is inseparable from an exquisitely intraindividual notion of ressentiment, which emerges from Nietzsche's vitalist and energetic concept of *power* and which is then taken up by Scheler. Individualist psychology does not assign a constituent role to the figure of the other in the life of each of us. The dependence on others is conceived above all as an external obstacle to the fulfilment of individual desires. The other is not perceived as a model to be imitated and therefore as a mimetic source of the desires that can become the target of ressentiment.

Our hypothesis does not lead us to deny the close relationship between ressentiment and modernity that was clearly shown by Nietzsche and taken over by Scheler in relation to bourgeois philanthropy rather than Christianity, but it calls into question the theoretical bases of the theses of the two German scholars. Both made the mistake of placing the root of ressentiment in men's will to power, ignoring the anthropological condition of reciprocal comparison that characterizes all human action.

A genealogy of ressentiment informed by the mimetic studies of Girard concentrates its attention on the image of this emotion as a social configuration that arises from envy and is consolidated in modern democratic institutions. Our ressentiment is not the flower that bloomed from a sick will to power, but the expression of a social configuration that takes shape from our reciprocal actions, that takes shape from the sense of frustration arising from the failures of daily competition, that is exacerbated by the progressive diffusion of an egalitarian tendency.

The secularization of Christianity in the form of modern democratic principles consolidated the idea of equality between men. In this sense, the revelation of the Gospels certainly precipitated the disappearance of the ordering power of violence, opening the gates to the explosion of the negative reciprocity of mimetic desire.

The diffusion of the idea of equality leads to a reduction of hierarchy and leads to an intensification of competition and rivalry between men, where in principle anyone can dominate anyone, where comparison with others is always more exposed to the risk of extreme competition.

The others, especially those who are secretly envied and admired, easily become rivals who humiliate and offend us, causing "justified" rancor that can be transformed into a struggle to abolish unfair privileges or into destructive reprisals against everybody who is "other than me."

But the mimetic genealogy of ressentiment, unlike the Nietzschean genealogy, shows that Christian revelation, the only true source of the modern deflagration of sacrificial orders, contains in its secularized forms a possible antidote to modern ressentiment.

Modern democratic institutions, by giving everyone a vote and subjecting every hierarchy to impersonal criteria, have removed from a few "great men" the privilege of deciding the destiny of all the others. Democracy has thus become a method of protecting our fragility as imperfect and incomplete men and not, as Nietzsche thought, a method for hiding our fragility and our meanness of spirit behind the mask of justice.

When Nietzsche constructs his story of morals, he unhesitatingly condemns Christian revelation. This decision leads him to delegitimize all modern institutional orders, which like modern democracy are ultimately founded on the revelation of the Gospels.

The contempt for ressentiment often hides a desire to exclude, because they are destined to feel ressentiment, those who are assumed to be fragile by definition. The opposite perspective assumes the Gospels' principles of preventing exclusion and of love for one's neighbor that are at the root of modern democratic orders.

All this is possible only if the new and radical image of man contained in the Gospels is made concrete. Christian revelation is the custodian of a new anthropological awareness, which shows the profound need for each person to be completed through the other; in this anthropological necessity we can see a possible shimmer of hope for a form of human coexistence that forgoes exclusion. Relationship with the other would then become an occasion for "resurrection" rather than the Dostoyevskian infernal warren of "undergrounds." This is because it is not ressentiment per se (in its presumed substance) that is the root of evil between humans, but rather a certain form of continuous and incessant exchange with the other, a certain form of relational processes. Oppression, exclusion, and the cruelest forms of barbarism are not the expression of a profound and intrinsically corrupting emotion such as ressentiment. They are a part of our way of coexisting, inside a wider framework of sense, that defines us together with the other and which also gives us the possibility of a search for pardon, even if it is wearisome and never definitively achieved.

This intense egalitarian tendency may well become a threat to the very democratic institutions that are based on it in the modern evangelical ethos.

The figure of the scapegoat in Girard's analysis is essential for understanding the matrix of the secularization process that is taking place in modern and contemporary society.[10] The Gospel revelation of sacrifice has opened up to men a paradoxical landscape in which hunting the scapegoat is increasingly visible and for this reason increasingly cruel. Our care for victims and for those who are excluded grows, as does our ability to recognize in the scapegoat an unjustly accused innocent victim. But this awareness does not restrain the search for scapegoats, which, because it is deprived of the ritual safety valves, takes on unexpected intensity in our society.

Democracy, and other secularized forms of Christianity, unlike what Nietzsche and Scheler would like, should not be morally condemned under the pretense that they are rooted in the ressentiment of a few sick individuals and are therefore clear signs of humanity's decadence. On the contrary, these social forms, as Girard has tried to show, have been a brake on the spread of uncontrolled competition and of rivalry in the period of the "death of God."

Since the mythical-ritual "mechanism" for generating social order has irremediably entered into a crisis through the revelation of the Gospels, modern and democratic institutions have played a key role in containing rivalry and reciprocal hatred between men.

The transformations taking place in the modern era, including democracy, far from being the result of the ressentiment of the weak against the strong, are the expression of the attempt to create nonsacrificial orders that take their inspiration from the Gospels' rule of not excluding the other and of not condemning our weaknesses.

The challenge for men and women of late modernity is to recognize a profound and radical tension between two contradictory tendencies that permeate our society: increasing attention to the excluded and to our own fragility on the one hand and toward persecutory mechanisms on the other hand. From this point of view, the history of democracy can be interpreted as the story of a continuous tension between our increasing compassion for potential victims and the persistence of persecutory situations, a sign that social exclusion cannot be eliminated just because it is becoming increasingly recognizable.

This is a powerful contradiction that is widely misunderstood by common wisdom, which leads us to view people of contemporary society as being divided against themselves. Each of us, more or less unconsciously, experiences the tensions that lacerate our society, such as the inevitable ressentiment, as mediocrity and the craze for power that inform our more customary relationships, and the desire to encourage democratic civil coexistence without resorting to expiatory and sacrificial shortcuts.

It is difficult to reconcile these contradictions into a stable harmonious whole because they threaten us at the intimate level. But the chance also exists of converting into a resource these obstacles that we strew on the path to our salvation. It will come from the awareness, progressively constructed, that the source of the intuitive ethos of the most far-reaching modern transformations is found in the Judeo-Christian tradition, which caused this undermining and which in a way also guides it.

6
Toward a Sociology of Ressentiment

O, when degree is shaked,
Which is the ladder to all high designs,
The enterprise is sick! How could communities,
Degrees in the schools and brotherhoods in cities,
Peaceful commerce from dividable shores,
The primogenitive and due of birth,
Prerogative of age, crowns, scepters, laurels,
But by degree, stand in authentic place?

—Shakespeare, *Troilus and Cressida*

An analysis of Nietzsche and of Scheler's definitions of ressentiment, filtered by Girard's mimetic theory, offers the social scientist the possibility of an explicative model of this specific emotion. It is a relational emotion that is generative of modern and contemporary social reality, at the same time it is generated by specific historic processes. The model is capable of highlighting the dynamic and circular nature of interactions between subjects from the micro to the macro levels, between intrapsychic events and social behavior.

The analysis of ressentiment in René Girard's theory shows that this emotion evolves from mimetic desire: it is an affective experience that people have when a rival denies them opportunities or valuable resources (including status) which they consider to be socially accessible. This emotion concerns simultaneously the social structures and the relationships in which actors are engaged. It is a specific figure of mimetic desire that is typical of contemporary society, where the equality that is proclaimed at the level of values contrasts with striking inequalities of power and access to material resources. This dichotomy generates increasing tension between highly competitive and egalitarian mimetic desires and growing social inequalities.

Girard refers to this evolution of mimetic desire as internal mediation, where social differentiation has practically disappeared, and the power of mimesis is most destructive.

Girard describes internal mediation and its social consequences in his first book: *Mensonge romantique et vérité Romanesque* (1961).[1] While the social distance between individuals gradually decreases, the mutual imitation of individual desires grows. In contemporary society, the transition from external mediation to internal mediation increases the person's illusion that he or she has a unique, autonomous, and individual desire, whereas actually differences among people are progressively disappearing. Everyone feels legitimated to compare him- or herself to others and to desire what the other has, independently of any distinction in terms of social role, job, or group of reference.

Society seems increasingly individualistic, but an analysis of mimetic ressentiment shows that an individualist mentality also arises from the logic that leads to ressentiment. People imagine realizing an individualistic and authentic desire when in reality everyone needs a mediator in order to find a new desire, a need that is increasingly exaggerated by the paradoxical combination between growing competition among equals and an equally rising social inequality. All are thus condemned to a fundamental dissatisfaction that leads to a desire that finds no rest.

Ressentiment is a symptom of internal mediation. It arises from the contemporary illusion of infinite freedom within a mimetic context. It is an invasive emotion that does not just affect private life, but also dominates the public sphere. Certain collective and social phenomena reflect the extent to which ressentiment arises from mimetic obsession. The possibility of different evolutionary outlets depends, not only on social interactions, but also on common sense in specific action contexts. A particular example of this social process in Northern Italy is the Lega Nord (Northern League) movement. As we shall see in the following section, Lega Nord is a specific phenomenon of victim-playing in a democratic Western society.

Victim-Playing

To understand Lega Nord's case study we need to explain the idea of "victim-playing." Victim-playing, according to

Girard,[2] is a mimetic strategy that seeks to legitimize claims to certain advantages solely on the basis of having suffered harm. It is a mystification of the legitimate claim of a victim seeking "fair" personal and social redress. It is a mimetic strategy that uses ressentiment and exploits fretful demands in a cynical competition.

In the long term, victim-playing is harmful because it denies the value of alterity by stripping people of their social responsibilities and of the power to solve their problems. Those who "play the victim" require the help and recognition of the other as an instrument. The desire to use the other is hidden behind a veil of piety; this attitude is increasingly the expression of a selfish person who is completely self-centered, ready to condemn a chaotic and hostile social environment and to transform the other into an instrument of self-realization.

The genesis of victim-playing, according to Girard, is reducible to a process of reversal of the idea of the victim. This can be understood as the "specific counter-productivity" of a universal victim culture. "Specific counter-productivity" is, Ivan Illich argued,[3] a negative social indicator of an internal involution of the cultural system that generates it. It is an undesired secondary effect, an illegitimate child of a determined sociocultural system that relates, in the case in question, to an extensive shift of the idea of the victim.

Never before has the term "victim" acquired such a wide meaning that it now extends far beyond the idea of death that had traditionally been associated with it. It no longer refers only to those who lost their life in a sacrifice or in a disaster or in a calamity, but also to any who, through no fault of their own, were in some way harmed by persons or circumstances or harmed themselves, albeit unconsciously. Or to those who are subject to the will of others, because they are in thrall to them and incapable of reacting. There are all kinds and types of victims: victims of the mass media, of the courts, of the oppressor state, of the wife or of the husband, of the boss, and, last but not least, victims of themselves.

If such an extension appears as excessive as it is fundamental, we at least need to agree on its origins. For some scholars, "concern for the victims" always existed, everywhere; for some others it appears with the rise of humanism and modern bourgeois philanthropy; for others, it is even more recent and arose in the 1960s after the first sociological investigations of victimization.

More frequently, the roots of this behavior have been traced to our Greek-Roman and Judeo-Christian heritage, albeit to differing extents. According to some scholars, the idea of "victim" was born in Greece and is due to Socrates, who through his death bore witness to the injustice of a political process: he accepted his condemnation, although it was unjust, in the name of a higher common good, the laws of the city. The sun of Athens burned away the fog of myth to demonstrate the value of a reasoning victim.[4]

It is certainly the case that, in the classic philosophical tradition, and especially in Socrates, we find marks of the victim, but this explanation remains too limited. At the very least, according to Girard,[5] this position needs to be complemented.

I shall not attempt here a cause-and-effect analysis and will limit myself to a reflection at the meta-level, more precisely on the mimetic social interactions that define the specific qualities of the notion of victim and its degeneration into victim-playing.

Roughly speaking, my hypothesis is that victim-playing is a radical and complex transformation of a long and gradual historical reworking of the revelation of the Gospels. The phenomenology of the development of the Lega Nord constitutes a specific illustration of this social process.

The revelation of the Gospels, as we have seen in the second part of this book when we analyzed René Girard's mimetic theory, constitutes the basis of our attention to victims, before the present evolution and the universal generalization of the condition of victim, through ressentiment.

In order to appreciate the exceptional character of this transformation, we need to place it in its historical context. When we speak of a "victim" we point toward at least two things: a sacred value and a person. On the one hand the moral being, the symbol of our highest values and the fruit of a historical and ideological transformation. On the other hand, the victim is an innocent who has suffered violence, persecution, or vendetta.

From this point of view, there are two types of society: one where the victim is sacred, which we can name a sacrificial society; in the other, the victim is viewed as innocent. In this case, we can talk of a postsacrificial society or of a society of ressentiment. In postsacrificial or ressentiment-based society, we can distinguish between at least two strategies for social action relative to victims: on the one hand, emancipation of victims from inequality, exclusion, and persecution and, on the other hand, exploiting the position of the victim to gain social advantages. This last strategy is what I call victim-playing.

The problem created by victim-playing is that of knowing how to distinguish, on a case-by-case basis, victim-playing from real victims. How is this transition made possible from one pole to its opposite, where the one is the negation of the other?

The Exceptional Transition: From Innocence to Victim-Playing

The sacrificial value of the notion of victim and the specific qualities associated with the notion have undergone an extraordinary semantic transformation that for some of us appears as an exceptional phenomenon in this history of human societies.

From being sacred, the victim has come to be universally recognized as an innocent person. This new vision is according to Girard due to the revelation of the Gospels, which extended the anthropological meaning of victim. Christ's Passion bore testimony to the innocence of the unjustly persecuted and uncovered what was for a long time hidden in the sacrificial social order.

There are many anthropological and sociological implications of the Gospel revelation. Even in sacrificial societies, members of society took care of one another, but this care applied only to the members of the group to which one belonged. There was no universal and abstract principle of the victim, in the sense in which we are accustomed to conceive it today. It was in the first Christian communities, for example, that hope and help were offered not only to the destitute of one's group but to *anybody* as a shelter from the afflictions of a decadent society.

During a long reworking of history that lasted twenty centuries the Gospel meaning of "innocent victim," which characterized the compassionate spirit of the first Christian communities, according to Girard, underwent a multitude of transformations. A further semantic shift over the last few decades has been toward what I previously called victim-playing.

The evolution of the idea of the victim highlights the fact that the cause of most human suffering is to be found in interactions, which from the very origin have been capable of generating victims, feeding and camouflaging antagonistic and destructive tensions in their midst.

The history of humankind, according to Girard, is a long chronicle of violence and injustice, slavery and exploitation, mostly related by the epics of the victors and the elegiac cantos of survivors. When humans did not succumb to disease, predators, and the forces of nature, they had to cope with abuses from their fellow humans. It is this struggle that human societies, both sacrificial and postsacrificial, continue to nurture in their breast, demonstrating that they are often incapable of responding to deep-rooted injustice.[6]

The causes of injustice among humans are too deeply rooted in the mimetic desires that shape our lives for us to be able to free ourselves, without false moralism, in seeking the real possibilities of social justice. For a long time, the solution to problems that were of our own making was to blame a scapegoat. Today, the solution has become to use the claim to be a victim as an accusation, as a weapon between rivals. We choose to "play the victim" because it is strategically useful to the realization of our desires, inasmuch as it increases visibility, by publicizing suffering and fragility. Victims, as we know from media studies, increase audience ratings and attract the attention of others, and siding with them can be useful for very selfish reasons.

We cannot examine here the multitude of historical and social processes that enter into the concrete dimensions of victim-playing. My thesis is that a specific phenomenology of ressentiment that defines the qualities of a concrete mimetic strategy of victim-playing is characteristic of the activities and history of the Lega Nord.

The Political Use of the Victim-Playing in Italian Society

The Lega Nord movement came into being at the end of the 1970s, in several regions of Northern Italy, particularly in Veneto, Lombardy, and, to a certain extent, Piedmont. Although it relates specifically to European regionalist traditions based on the ideal of being autochthonous,[7] the strength of the popular consensus behind it derives from several phenomena present in those Italian regions: *anti-meridionalismo* (hostility to Southern Italy),[8] antistatism and the economic divide between the north and the south of the country, especially with regard to the Northeast.

Toward the end of the 1990s, this localism and the demand for an ethnic identity for the "northern people" situated in the mythical "Padania" also became a way to channel the growing racism relating to the immigration of non-EU citizens that, at that time, was turning into an unheard-of social phenomenon, in terms of both the quantity of flows, with respect to the recent past, and the cultural and political debate to which it gave rise.[9]

The Lega Nord movement's program is simple, populist,[10]

and opportunistic: it demands federalism in order to achieve multiple objectives of an economic nature: the dismantling of the social welfare state, the reduction of fiscal pressure, and deregulation. The aim is to free the country's productive social forces from the seemingly most inactive social figures: trade unionists, politicians, public officials, and so on.

In order to understand Lega Nord it is undoubtedly important to interpret the social changes that have taken place in Western countries and in Italy, from the crisis of class relations to the birth of a new population of medium and small businessmen, from migratory flows to the crisis of the welfare system, and so on.[11] But it is just as important to comprehend the emotional tone of the movement, the deep-rooted bond between the Lega Nord and the sentiment that is common to many northern citizens. The deep-rooted foundations of *leghismo* cannot be understood unless we recognize its great ability to make a political use of Northern Italy's victim-playing.

The Lega Nord

In Italian society, the economic boom of the 1980s generated widespread affluence, especially in the Northeast. This had been in the past a poor agricultural area with high illiteracy from which people emigrated. The agricultural past of Northeastern Italy and its rapid and recent transformation into an industrial economy based on small and medium enterprises[12] have intensified the dynamics of ressentiment. Rapid economic success seemed to promise a future of permanent well-being and unlimited freedom. However, the subsequent economic crises of the 1990s created significant social disparities between citizens, as well as an unexpected aversion toward public institutions, which were represented as detached and uninterested in "the real problems of the people."

Closing the borders of one's local community initially became the terrain upon which rested the attempt to build a new neoliberal and antistatist political project, the pillar of which was the principle of the war between us and them. The community of the "we" is represented by a multitude of dynamic and independent individuals who identify with the common ressentiment toward all those (public administrators, immigrants, rival economies) who impede or threaten the success of individuals who live in search of self-fulfillment. The aim is to free the country's active and productive forces from the state's "fetters and constraints" and from all those who hinder development.[13]

The Italian politician Umberto Bossi, leader of Lega Nord, is a particularly apt subject for an analysis of a political activity that attempts to exploit the conflicting forces of ressentiment. Umberto Bossi was born in 1941 to a Northern Italian middle-class family. After obtaining an electronics diploma from the Radio Elettra correspondence school, he enrolled at the University of Pavia, where he studied medicine for a couple of years. Abandoning his studies before graduating, he began a brief career as a singer with the stage name "Donato." In an interview, his first wife, Gigliola Guidali, says she asked for a divorce after discovering that her husband had never graduated, despite the fact that he left the house every morning with his doctor's bag and the words, "Goodbye darling, I'm off to the hospital." He had failed to take eleven examinations and did not write his graduation thesis. In 1961, he took part in the Festival of Castrocaro, where he and his group were eliminated. He therefore decided to abandon his musical career and, at the beginning of the 1980s, began to dedicate his time to politics, which became his main interest. Between 1974 and 1975 he was a card-carrying member of the then Italian Communist Party of Verghera, Samarate division. In that period, he also spent a few months selling paintings to raise funds to support the Chilean victims of Augusto Pinochet. In their 2004 book dedicated to the incredible story of this politician, Giampiero Rossi and Simone Spina[14] write that he was attracted to politics from an extremely early age, taking part in the student movement of 1968 and serving, in rapid succession, in the communist group "Il Manifesto," the extreme-left Party of Proletarian Unity (PDUP), the left-wing Catholic workers' association, and the Greens.

His personal and professional story is one that he shares with many Italians from the provinces and of humble origins who seek social fulfillment in a radically opportunistic form of pragmatism. Nonetheless, these biographical events only partly explain his future political success, which makes an original and unique use of the force of ressentiment. Analyzing a speech made by Umberto Bossi during a party political broadcast on the occasion of political talks on 27 and 28 March 1994 and of a speech broadcasted by RAI DUE, will enable us to interpret the salient traits of a then nascent ideology that is now the cultural framework of a significant social bloc present in a large part of the country. This is a transcript of the speech:

> Dear electors: in a few hours' time we will vote
> to choose the political powers that will have to
> govern the country in the coming years. The main
> problems in this country, problems that are a syn-
> thesis of many other problems, are the enormous
> national debt, which conditions every national
> economic choice, and the spread of organized
> crime throughout the land. Without doubt, the
> parties have some responsibility, not only for not
> having made the reforms that should have been
> made, but also for not even guaranteeing to make
> them in the future. For example, with regard to

the national debt, they have announced that, if they win, everything will continue as before. That is to say, they will increase taxes, instead of cutting down on waste and reducing costs. It is clear that the parties' interpretation of the word "waste" is different from our own. For the parties of the regime, "waste" means buying votes, guaranteeing electoral consensus. It is for this reason that we are unable to escape, that we are prisoners in a vicious circle that sees more taxes, more waste, more unlawfulness throughout the land and an increase in the intermingling of the mafia, criminal organizations, and politics. It is for this reason that the mafia cannot be overcome, that it cannot be defeated by the police and magistrates. The mafia is politics. Therefore, a political act is needed to defeat it: in the polling booth we must choose a political force that is also a great moral force. I know only Lega Nord, a party praised by the international press, which clearly depicts and presents us as the only Italian political power with a plan for real change in the country. Therefore, vote Lega Nord, for the Chamber and the Senate, remembering that in the central and southern regions we are listed as "Lega Nord—Centro-Sud."

This apparently innocuous speech by Umberto Bossi, who was a senator in the previous legislature, reveals, in fact, with extraordinary clarity how the consensus he is seeking is fueled by the ressentiment diffused throughout the North. An analysis of the categories of this televised speech reveals some of the salient traits of this nascent libertarian and intrinsically ideological political project.

THE CORRUPTION OF THE ECONOMY

The country is distinguished by a series of undefined problems. The "problems that are a synthesis of many other problems," according to Bossi's formula, are the national debt and the mafia. The governing classes would appear to be shirking all past and future responsibilities, as they are accomplices of collusion between an abstract, highly financial economy and the concrete interests of a criminal nature (waste, the buying and selling of votes and favors). This image of a corrupt political class and an economy that is not based on productivity is an attempt to find a cause far from everyday inequalities and the real social relationships, which are becoming increasingly fragmented. The corruption of the economy is one of the most effective arguments for constructing a consensus. This was because "Mani Pulite"[15] was active during those years. The expression "Mani Pulite" refers to a period of the 1990s characterized by a series of nationwide investigations by judges of politicians, of the economy, and of Italian institutions. The investigations brought to light a system of giving and soliciting bribes and illegal funding of parties at the highest levels of Italian politics and finance. This phenomenon was known as "Tangentopoli" (Bribesville). Ministers, deputies, senators, entrepreneurs, and even former prime ministers were involved. The investigations were initially conducted by a group of magistrates from the Milan Public Prosecutor's Office (consisting of the magistrates Antonio Di Pietro, Piercamillo Davigo, Francesco Greco, Gherardo Colombo, Tiziana Parenti, and Ilda Boccassini, and headed by the public prosecutor Francesco Saverio Borrelli and his assistant, Gerardo D'Ambrosio), but they were then extended to the whole of Italy.[16] The investigations made the public very indignant, and Lega Nord emerged as the movement that expressed this indignation.

THE CONSPIRACY OR SCAPEGOAT THEORY

"Mani Pulite" reveals the desire to accuse the governing class of all the faults of capitalism's cyclical crises. This conspiracy theory is based on the conviction that power is in the hands of an inner circle that prevents the country's vital forces, the self-employed and self-employed lower middle class, from finding space for self-fulfillment and influencing the political choices of a corrupt governing class. The apparent banality of Bossi's proposal hides the ressentiment against the "caste": the governing class from which one repeatedly awaits the necessary solution and which becomes the privileged scapegoat upon which to lay the blame for the growing failures caused by embitterment in every sphere of competitive public and private life.

This competitive life clashes with growing social inequalities, creating a general feeling of discrepancy. The disaggregating effects of growing competitive relationships have intensified, in particular with the decline of the welfare state.[17] The progressive loss of the protections provided by the system of social services of the nation-state produces unequal social conditions. The social condition of action is characterized by this heightening of inequalities. In Western societies, whose wealth cannot be compared with any other human community, what could be called the "dark side" of well-being develops constantly. The advantages of technology, of mass production, of scientific and technological progress, and of medicine have made the lives of people in the West enviable for most of the earth's inhabitants. However, access to resources, knowledge, and opportunities remains seriously unequal, and in many cases the gap is widening, not only between the North and South, but also within the opulent societies of the North.[18]

The increase in social and economic disparities combines with the ideological and cultural tendency toward equality in desires, making daily interactions extremely frustrating, because in ceaseless real and virtual mutual comparisons, each person feels entitled to the same opportunities as others, to the same desires, to the same ambitions, all of which clash with the reality of radically unequal starting points. The illusion of individual liberty, which rules unchallenged at the ideological level, together with the proclaimed infinite possibilities of choice, clash with the concrete feasibility of action. Contemporary society is egalitarian at the level of the values it proclaims, but is radically unequal not only in terms of the large differences in power between the elite and the masses, but also in terms of a new increasing inequality in the actual possession of wealth.[19]

Those who want to share in prosperity, and in the free style of life that comes with it, have to clear the very difficult hurdle of meeting all the requirements for accessing the market, before making the right and most advantageous choice. The result is the entrenchment of ressentiment in a paradoxical social relationship: on the one hand the social actor is pressured and urged to participate in a kind of Toyland where everyone is equal, free to desire unlimited educational consumption and self-realization opportunities;

on the other hand the social actor is rigidly constrained by the actual possibilities and the constantly possible rebuff from mimetic comparison with others. The Lega Nord polarizes this general feeling of discrepancy with the governing class, upon which it lays the blame for the growing number of failures.

MORALIZATION

The establishment does not deserve the social reputation that it is usually granted; it is hypocritical, it hides behind a false decorum. Therefore what is needed is a political force that is also a moral force. However, the causes of social injustice are too deeply rooted in the structure in which we live for us to free ourselves from them with false moralism. For a long time, the strategy of the scapegoat has been the magic and violent solution to problems, which we ourselves tend to generate, more or less consciously. In the discourse of the Lega Nord movement, the solution or at least strategy is false moralism, which is used as a weapon between rivals. One chooses to "be moral" when it is strategically advantageous to do so because it increases visibility, according to a hypo-critical process that hides the power of a political ruling class, whose various sections alternatively governed the country over the last twenty years. This is well known by those who turn moralism into a product of dramatization, in order to lay claim to rights or simply discredit an adversary.

In this moralization operates the principle, theorized by Carl Schmitt, of the dichotomy between friend and enemy.[20] There is a large body of sociological literature that reveals the primary importance of the dualistic approach that lies at the basis of the distinction between in and out, between the in-group and the out-group, on which linguis-tic, cultural, and religious barriers and so on can be erected. On the basis of these barriers individuals and groups then construct the datum of the biological, religious, cultural, ethic difference, which justifies hostility to our adversary, whoever he or she may be, Jewish, Gypsy, black, and so on, and the "irrepressible force" of prejudices is unleashed in the minds of persecutors.

The dichotomy between friend and enemy acts as an identity operator. It performs a function of social integration and of internal solidarity. In this way, it allows the diverging interests of multiple actors (social classes, corporations, workers) and the internal variety of civil society to coexist in a political, cultural, and social unity. The political opposition between friend and enemy has a unifying force because it also performs a function of sublimation for internal mimetic conflicts. When social agents realize that their socioeconomic condition depends on their choices as well as on those of other actors, and that it is not dictated by a transcendent and immutable order, then the conviction also takes shape that it is possible to modify their social condition. Social tensions caused by economic or political crises, by negative reciprocity—in short, by envy and rivalry within society— can be projected by Lega Nord onto the enemy and polarized against the corrupt establishment.

VICTIMIZATION

The theme of victim-playing is crucial. We need to stress the expression "We are prisoners," which indicates the condition of Umberto Bossi's targeted electorate as victims. Italians appear to be victims of collusion between the corrupt upper echelons of the establishment and the malignant base of society, that is, widespread delinquency and the mafia. The victimization stirred up by the Lega Nord movement requires an instrumental use of those who consider themselves superior or privileged: it is a discourse that increasingly is an expression of an individual enclosed within himself or herself, in his or her own hypertrophic narcissism. In the 1980s, it became a style of life, ready to condemn a chaotic and hostile social environment and transform other individuals into instruments for the atonement of that for which all share the blame. In the long run, and this is the most politically distressing aspect, victimization negates the value of alterity, as it robs people of their civil and social responsibilities and, even more importantly, of their power to resolve their problems actively. A critical analysis of victim-playing reveals the unpalatable truth that social justice requires people to take responsibility for their joint participation in the complex system of relations that constitute society, where nobody in particular is more responsible than anybody else.

The Lega Nord has now been part of the country's government for approximately twenty years and has directly governed some of its regions continuously. This suggests an extension to our analysis to three other characteristics of the Lega Nord's political discourse.

The first characteristic concerns the question of social mobility and merit. During the 1980s, the problem of personal merit and its relation to the social conditions of agents became increasingly acute in Italian society. Umberto Bossi and the *leghista* movement fueled the belief that an inner circle of people possessing an enormous amount of power used "dishonest" means to hold back and marginalize those below them who were aspiring to greater social prestige. This belief was justified at that time, however, by the action of magistrates with regard to Tangentopoli. The growing distance between the governing class and the multitude of individuals is in this discourse combined with the injustice of denied recognition due to the lack of respect for a "true" hierarchy (of the meritocratic variety), which is invoked by the neoliberal principle of widespread competition for the victory of the best. The Lega Nord movement presents itself as a political force that will finally be able to resolve this fundamental social injustice: that Italian society is not always able to optimize its best resources.

A second characteristic of the Lega Nord's ressentiment is local prejudice. Localism is a logical consequence of the scapegoat theory. The Italian lower middle and middle classes imagine themselves imprisoned by the centralist bureaucracy of the nation-state, which has proved itself unable to guarantee the necessary social protection to this segment of the population. The small- and medium-sized craft companies and freelance professionals feel betrayed by the state, which does not fully implement the country's modernization plan, due to an enormous national debt. The social protection system was the price to pay in exchange for economic progress, but the plan was implemented from the center toward the periphery, and from top to bottom, thus taking the focus away from local specificities. The Lega Nord's promise to return to prioritizing local, rather than central, political life became a way to channel the frustration caused by the national elites' failed realization of a future of continuous success. It ably hides the fact that a large part of the economic success of small- and medium-sized companies was favored by widespread tax evasion and, in some cases, by the corruption of local politicians.

Lastly, we have the *problem of consensus*. An ideology of ressentiment must face an unavoidable problem: the more it gains consensus, the more powerful it becomes, and the more it also becomes similar to the political culture that is the target of its anger.[21] Accordingly, it can only manage to remain credible by systematically distracting its electorate from its political actions and positions, concentrating attention, rather, on its moral intentions. Therefore, it will always be others who hinder the realization of a necessary and pressing future project. The leaders, on the other hand, will be asked to give expression to their ill feeling and their own personal negative impulses, displaying how close they are to the common ressentiment.

The problems of consensus, mobility, and merit and local prejudice are three critical aspects of the Lega Nord's policy that have evolved further since the beginning of the global economic crisis in 2008. Current economic and social transformations in Italy are undergoing a critical evolution in the north of the country.[22]

Ressentiment is increasing, and Lega Nord is no longer able to channel the discontent of the country's most significant areas. In the 2013 general election, Lega Nord's share of the vote fell dramatically.

Lega Nord started to face difficulties when it became clear that uncontrolled spending by the state could no longer ensure consensus, simply because the state could no longer financially afford to continue such a policy, and it also became clear that depriving Italy of its sinecures, privileges, and abuses or simply cutting back on the benefits to which people had grown accustomed was impossible. The promises, first to free Northern Italy from the "oppression of the robbers in Rome," second to reorganize public administration on a federal basis according to merit and efficiency, and finally to review the catastrophic governance of the Italian regions, were not maintained. The Lega Nord did not keep its word and got caught up itself in the corruption that it denounced.[23]

The Lega Nord began to realize just how difficult it is to change from the inside the relationship between the citizens and the state. In order to break out of this increasingly suffocating deadlock, to convince Italian society of something of which it could never have been convinced otherwise, the Lega Nord turned its populist propaganda against the immigrant minorities, marking them as potential scapegoats.

Lega Nord is a movement driven by ressentiment that has taken part in governing Italy for twenty years without managing to maintain the promises made to its electors. In this manner, ressentiment has turned against Lega Nord itself, especially in the Veneto Region, where its share of the vote has fallen from 26.05 percent to 11 percent. Many of Umberto Bossi's voters were prepared to overlook his faux pas, the corruption of the ruling class, in return for federalism, for solutions to the problems posed by the economic crisis, a concrete strategy of support for people in the face of European and global competition. Initially, Lega Nord seemed to be a new movement that was hostile to the political power of the moment, that got the votes of traditionally nonparticipating members of the electorate, and that provided an outlet for anger and frustration. After twenty years of misrule it found itself caught up in the same logic and dynamics of bribery and corruption that were the object of its political denunciations.

For twenty years, Northern Italy has displayed its social and cultural malaise, above all through its support for Lega Nord, which expressed the interests of regional territories. After these twenty years of misrule, the North's ressentiment has evolved again and has turned against the entire political world and its institutions. Politicians are accused of being too remote from the real problems of citizens, of being unable to solve the problems of productive development, and of being hostile to small and medium enterprises. The Northern Italy question has in the meantime changed: the North is now in grave financial and economic difficulties, like the rest of the world's advanced economies. Ressentiment is taking the form of inward-looking resignation that exacerbates the victim-playing strategy that is already inherent in Lega Nord.

7
From Victim-Playing to the Ethics of Ressentiment

"Scandal" means, not one of those ordinary obstacles that we avoid easily after we run into it the first time, but a paradoxical obstacle that it is almost impossible to avoid: the more this obstacle, or scandal, repels us, the more it attracts us. Scandals are responsible for the false infinity of mimetic rivalry.... They secrete increasing quantities of envy, jealousy, resentment, and hatred—all the poisons most harmful not only for the initial antagonist but also for all who become fascinated by their rivalistic desires.

—René Girard, *I See Satan Fall Like Lightning*

Victim-playing, as by the *leghismo*, does not exhaust the questions raised by the word *ressentiment*. Like any other human manifestation of mimesis, this interaction is also fraught with contradictions and ambivalence that also provide positive possibilities.

We are living through decisive metamorphoses of interactive dynamics, metamorphoses that involve a high risk of heightening conflicts between unlimited desires and limited opportunities, leading to a crystallization of many forms of experience into ressentiment.

Ressentiment, the child of egalitarianism on the one hand and of free competition on the other, is thus inseparable from the set of values and principles that we call democratic. In fact, who could fail to also recognize behind the desire for equality a desire to put everyone on the same level or simply the fear of downward mobility? Are the men and women in societies with universal rights therefore doomed to suffer perennial ressentiment toward one another, toward society, as well as political, institutional, and religious authorities? Should they rebel against the principles of universal legality that have triumphed in the modern era, rebel against the dull and gray morality of an egalitarianism that stifles the expression of "free spirits," as various reactionary political and religious movements suggest with depressing regularity?

Following the diagnosis so far made, it may appear that late modernity has willy-nilly reached an important crossroad: men and women must either remain trapped in an unhealthy desire for revenge, or they must free themselves of the democratic principles of equality that justify a culture of mediocrity and fuel ressentiment—unless they, perhaps, want to revive the idea of revolution, based on the promise of a radiant future that is simultaneously egalitarian and brimming over with prosperity, and where hate is directed against a "class enemy," who in any case is doomed by history to succumb eventually.

However, the inevitability of this crossroad is only apparent. Although the egalitarian constraints of democracy and the aspiration to the equal dignity of the desires of all may constitute an inexhaustible propellant for ressentiment, it remains true that the injustices caused by inequalities constitute an equally good propellant that cannot be dismissed as mere ressentiment. An insidious underground is found lurking behind demands for social justice, but this does not automatically mean that all requests for justice lose legitimacy. In "A Mimetic Reading of Helmut Shoeck's Theory of Envy," Paul Dumouchel[1] argued that mimetic ressentiment is but a moment in a process of mimetic conflict, a process in which we all participate at times. It is a shifting position that anyone can occupy, rather than an essence.

Ressentiment, as I have tried to argue in these pages, is not fueled so much by egalitarianism as by the tension between acute expectations of equality and structural inequalities.

The systemic antagonism between "formal social parity" and "major *de facto* differences in power" outlined by Scheler, and the mimetic nature of desire, which Girard describes as boundless rivalry between desires that imitate one another, do not configure static or negative, but rather ambivalent, social and communicative conditions that are dynamically open to a variety of outcomes. The contradictions that exist among them can also help us identify openings to new forms of experience and cohabitation that are capable of transforming the failures, the fears of mimetic comparison, and the "sad passions" of ressentiment into new horizons of solidarity and into new creative possibilities.[2]

Living in a new space of critical action in the age of ressentiment means learning to live within one's limits, with one's own fragility, and with the insurmountable fact that one is part of interactive relationships, as well as of larger constraining games of mimetic reflection.

Stories and personal suffering become mixed in biographies, and then mixed again with the biographies of other people; situational and institutional contradictions flow in and out of people's lives, often breaking the circle of solitude. When we are victim of an injustice we inevitably feel the need to find someone who is responsible, who is the culprit: we look for somebody, the enemy, the foreigner, the system. The humiliated person discovers that he or she depends on the others who have offended her or him and depends on their often refused acknowledgment.[3] Powerlessness in the face of the wrong suffered immediately becomes a reason for anxiety, but it can also be transformed into an occasion for openness toward what is new.

From faulty decisions, from one's own, and from others' failures, we can learn important lessons about our identity and the possibility of a future that does not mechanically repeat the past. One can above all learn to recognize the self-delusion of those who hide to varying degrees behind forms of victim-playing, remaining increasingly trapped in the secret delights of ressentiment.

When we learn to recognize in ourselves and in others the paradoxical dynamics of ressentiment, to which we are all inevitably exposed, we can also denounce the privileges and inequalities of power, of wealth, and of control that prevent the spread of cooperation, that stifle solidarity, and identify the changes required to promote equality and equal opportunity without, contrary to what Nietzsche thought, unequivocally condemning ourselves to the morality of mediocrity and ressentiment.

In *Le Retour de l'acteur* Alain Touraine[4] wrote about the children and grandchildren of Nazis in West Germany. Young Germans, full of shame for what the Nazis state was, and full of ressentiment for the silence of older generations during the postwar period, took part in the pacifist movement of 1968, and this participation surely has numerous implications. This profound crisis that marked an entire generation of Germans was also an opportunity to search for a form of cohabitation that was fairer and more cohesive. The transformations that were possible in those tragic historical conditions may be an example to follow, to turn into something positive the radical transformations facing men and women in today's society.

The experience of ressentiment that takes shape in the midst of dynamic interpersonal and intrapersonal social conflicts is necessarily extremely complex. More than a mere feeling of subjective and communicative frustration is at stake, however; it also opens up the difficult possibility of a transition to new personal and social competences and toward new forms of cooperation and collaboration.

The Ethics of Ressentiment

In the dynamics that lead to ressentiment, the boundary between good and evil is ambivalent. For example, insult and humiliation only take on a specific meaning within the reciprocal relationship between the insulter and the insulted. Humiliation and insult both depend on the fact that between the two people, the insulter and the insulted, a deep mimetic link is created: no individual would be able to humiliate us if we did not also admire him in a more or less veiled way, if we did not perceive him to be a model. In other words, ressentiment depends on the type of mimetic bond forged with the other, on the secret bond among persons.

But how is it then possible to transform hate into love? Is it possible to transform ressentiment into forgiveness without remaining, as Nietzsche would say, trapped in a masked desire for revenge? A comparison with the definition of ressentiment proposed by the Jewish intellectual Jean Améry in his reflections on his experiences as a prisoner in Auschwitz provides valuable help in critically examining this delicate topic.

In his comments on Améry's work, Roberto Esposito emphasized Améry's need for an ethics of ressentiment. The torment of being a victim is viewed as providing the basis for constructing an ethics that bear witness to this torment. In other words, according to Esposito, this ethics should constitute a "firm and solitary claim, on the need to meet without end what it is not possible to cancel."[5]

Améry presents ressentiment as a protest against forgiveness, because forgiveness risks vindicating the triumph of crime over spirit. But he constructs his own idea of ethics on a concept different from that expressed by the Nietzschean criticism of Christianity. Here is his cogent argument: "My resentments are there in order that the crime become a moral reality for the criminal, in order that he be swept into the truth of his atrocity."[6]

Améry's analysis dwells on the counterintuitive idea that ressentiment, as a way of reminding the persecutor of the criminal nature of his misdeed, is considered as a moral duty. Améry suggests the hypothesis that, inside an interactive context, "saying that one is resentful" or "showing ressentiment" can also be a way of communicating to those around us the gravity of a profoundly unjust insult. Viewed in this light, feeling ressentiment is not simply evil per se; it is not uniquely a degrading sentiment, but is also the expression of a painful transition between the private and the public: the duty not to forget the harm that people can do to one another. Améry raises the notion of ressentiment to the level of a moral instance that is necessary in order not to forget the crime committed: feeling ressentiment takes the form of a painful moral awareness of the impossibility of canceling the evil that has been done.

Améry's intellectual search reflects a decision to deny the possibility of forgiveness. It incarnates the painful awareness that sometimes the crime suffered is so grievous that one, not only does not want to forgive, but humanly must not forgive. For those who are trapped in a condition of extreme, absolute, and radical pain that can lead to self-destruction, asserting one's own ressentiment publicly can constitute the condition of release.

Améry's reflections should be considered as a valuable contribution to understanding how it is possible to transform ressentiment into a search for forgiveness by clearly and acutely highlighting the ambivalent nature of ressentiment.

In a mimetic context, an individual consciously receives and perceives only a small part of what surrounds and involves him or her: the other and relations with the other remain a mystery beyond his or her grasp. In such a condition, ressentiment can constitute both an expression of the destructive logic of violence and a strong public denunciation of the destructive power of evil. However, the outcome of this relationship, that is, which of the two processes will prevail, is a question that depends on the reciprocal coordination between the actors in question, and not on the presumed substantial good or evil value of ressentiment per se.

This ambivalent dimension of ressentiment obliges us to rigorous reflection in the search for forgiveness as an antidote to ressentiment. This search is not straightforward; its character can always change into its opposite, and it is never above suspicion. Forgiveness, if analyzed in the wider context of interactions between mimetic actors, and not only in the separate compartment of the individual conscience of the person who is forgiving, constitutes, like any other human experience, an action whose effects are ambivalent. Forgiving cannot a priori ensure a nonviolent issue to the interaction within which it intervenes. The forgiven person may in fact misconstrue my forgiving to such a point that he sees it as an opportunity to make oblivion triumph over memory and crime over justice.[7]

From a mimetic and relational point of view, Améry's

reflections illustrate the need to rethink the decision to forgive by grasping its irreducible complexity and ambivalence. In relational terms, it does not represent a way of forgetting crime; rather it is a necessary step on the way of *starting* to forgo the logic of rivalry and bullying, of humiliation and insult. In order to be effective, the decision to forgive must not, however, lose sight of the fact that it requires continuous incessant research that is not destined to succeed and is always exposed to the risk, mentioned by Améry, that of facilitating the triumph of oblivion.

In addition to the danger, identified by Améry, of forgiveness being transformed into forgetfulness, a second risk must also be borne in mind, which is intrinsic to the relational nature of communicative interaction. To the extent that forgiveness is a complex choice, in a scenario of fierce rivalry between individuals, it is sufficient for the other to construe my action as being underhand for it to really become so. No action can a priori be excluded from this possibility, not even forgiveness. This aspect of human relations makes the choice of forgiveness anything but simple and straightforward.[8] It must also not be forgotten that the action of forgiveness, understood as forgoing the process of competition, rivalry, and conflict can be read as a surreptitious challenge, as in the case of victim-playing, thus feeding the very process that it is trying to overcome. The comparison with the other always has a component of rivalry, and not even forgiveness can claim to be free from it: a simple look of renunciation, if interpreted by the rival as a sign of superiority, may be considered to be the same as a proud and arrogant gesture of challenge.

Choosing forgiveness requires boldness and prudence. Awareness of the fact that evil and violence between people are the result of our way of interacting is difficult to achieve and never completely achieved. If we choose forgiveness, it is not sufficient to think that this self-critical consciousness suffices to lead the relationship unilaterally to a nonviolent outcome. To forgive, we need the boldness of those who do not give up loving and the prudence of those who are aware of how difficult and complex relations with one's neighbor are.

The search for fraternity can be undertaken only together with the other: seeking reconciliation through forgiveness is possible only by accepting the difficult knowledge that the outcome of the relationship in the moment following forgiveness will depend decisively on the action of our neighbor. The search for forgiveness is a renunciation that leaves the last word to the other.

The Continuous Search for Fraternity

The suffering with which ressentiment is imbued prevents indifference and oblivion from spreading in relationships with those to whom we are close. Crisis, as Edgar Morin writes, is always an awakening. And because it is an "infected memory," ressentiment prevents any form of forgetting.[9] Suffering can lie awake in the darkest and deepest zones of ressentiment, in the Dostoyevskian underground, in the desire for a new bond of trust. The feeling of impotence behind ressentiment can be triggered in those who experience it by the mere lament and search for new, even radical, possibilities of justice, sometimes leading to innovative personal and social actions compared to the existing order.

Ressentiment is a destructive energy that, as Nietzsche argued, has often revealed all its explosive force in history, but at the same time it is a creative energy that from suffering can generate a tension that sets out to rethink the institutional devices that regulate common life.

René Girard has shown that projecting the causes of unease caused by the spread of menacingly rival interactions onto a scapegoat located outside of daily relationships was for thousands of years the most effective means of restoring the social order in times of crisis. This is a device that was long guaranteed by symbolic and mythical-sacred structures, and in the last few centuries, in modern societies, by symbolic and organizational structures based on the authority of the nation-state. Today, however, with the rapid weakening of the symbolic order promised and instituted by modernity, and with the emergence of the global era that is devoid of a universally recognized symbolic apex, this device can no longer be as effective in guaranteeing the criteria of inclusion and exclusion, the cultural bases of identity, the credibility of the promises of justice, the rules for resolving conflicts, and not even the principle of the state's monopoly of violence, as global terrorism shows.[10] This is the reason why the desire for self-affirmation turns into widespread disappointment and ressentiment. Competition, in the name of the modern value of self-realization, has been so intensified and amplified on the planetary scale that no "venting" on a scapegoat located in a clearly certifiable exterior can resolve the cause of the widespread unease produced by competition.

But it is precisely from the bitterness of disappointment and the impotence that spread in people's minds because of the failure of the modern promise, that a new awareness can be born. Certainly, this awareness to which Améry bore witness is not very widespread. Solitude and indifference too often seem to dominate.[11]

Nevertheless, from defeat a rethinking can take place in our understanding of cohabitation that is so deeply rooted in the principles of individual power, of exhausting competition, and of social engineering—principles conceived in another time, within an ideology of progress whose Promethean promises of control of nature and of time have long concealed the daily truth of reciprocal interdependence.

As the standardizing and regulating force of the welfare

state and of the modern symbolic order associated with it decline, not only is it the case that insecurity increases, and that mutual competition intensifies, but previously inhibited potentials also emerge. The obviousness of many normative constraints that prevent individuals from building up relationships based on collaboration and solidarity decline.[12] At all levels of life, local and planetary, we increasingly witness the impossibility of leading a self-referenced and solipsistic life.

In this period of crisis, ressentiment has two faces. On the one hand, it seems to condemn us to isolate ourselves and to compete in an unbridled manner. The current ideology of the right to self-realization increases barbarous rivalries and the fear of failure. When the social role of the other is or can be discounted, everyone can assert against others the legitimacy of all or any of his or her desires. This condemnation, however, is only being inflicted upon those who do not accept their own intimate and constituent relationship with the other, who reject the truth of social interdependence and choose the path of individual self-affirmation. On the other hand, and at the same time, ressentiment is an explosive reserve of radical criticism of the existing social and symbolic order, of social and institutional organizations, fossilized in forms inherited from modernity, that are unable to promote a relationship between individuals who accept one another in their singularity and fragility, rather than in their presumed self-referencing self-sufficiency. Recognizing the dual nature of ressentiment is the first step toward searching for the new forms of democratic cooperation and participation that we need to imagine, no matter how difficult they may be to identify.

Current transformations are providing individuals with great opportunities for personal, professional, and cultural growth, and also with new major responsibilities. These unparalleled transitions give grounds to the hope that the project of fairer cohabitation is possible.

For scientists who wish to contribute to the evolving transformation of the spreading unease in social interactions by favoring the emergence of processes of collaboration, ample space is opening up for research into the possible criteria and tools for promoting reciprocal trust and confidence in a better future, promoting the use a decisive key word, *fraternity*,[13] alongside, of course, the historical democratic principles of equality and liberty, but with a new urgency brought to the forefront by the dynamics of late-modern ressentiment that are discussed here.

The growth in the awareness of the disquiet of the citizens of the global society is not only the result of scandalous inequalities, not only the result of old and new "unfreedoms" that beset social interaction, but also of our manner of staging our daily interdependence, of the way we present ourselves to one another. It is a hard-won awareness, one that is never sufficiently gained, that can never be translated into an automatic response that does not require responsibility to be activated. It requires social research into the emotional and cultural dynamics from which this awareness emerges and where also is the latent danger, intrinsic to global society, of causing violent conflicts, of initiating processes of exclusion, of marginalization, or of hunting for new scapegoats. This research should at the same time indicate new ways of participating in the construction of a form of cohabitation that is, as far as possible, fraternal.[14]

The appeal to fraternity should not be confused with an

appeal to benevolence. If the feeling of fraternity is to make headway, the benevolence of one's intentions can never be assumed to provide a sufficient guarantee that one can unequivocally implement behaviors that produce cooperative and reconciliatory human relations. In other words, we must acknowledge an inescapable paradox that is constitutive of the action of reconciliation; the best intentions can also favor the worst of consequences. Fraternity implies a continuous exploration that is only constructed together with the other, and especially together with the rival other: reconciliation is only possible by accepting that the outcome of the relationships always decisively also depends on the action of the other person, on an unforeseeable concatenation of actions and reactions, which no good intentions are sufficient to direct toward a cooperative outcome and a reciprocal acknowledgment in difference.[15] It is necessary to "mean well," but it is not sufficient. We must also accept that actions will be measured by the other on the basis of their effects, not only on the basis of their intentions. When we act only trusting in our own good intentions, we inevitably negate the reciprocal dimension of relationship. The possibilities of the fraternal relationship are thus lost, canceled by the pretended linearity of the relation between intention and its effects.

Fraternity constitutes a founding principle of democratic coexistence, which stems from the best anthropological presuppositions of the West. Proclaimed over two hundred years ago by the French Revolution, it is linked to Christian charity and reveals the secularized message of the Gospels, the set of democratic principles that were affirmed during modernity.[16] In many ways of course, the principle of fraternity is as old as humankind.[17] But in archaic cultures it was normally only practiced toward members of one's own community, clan, or group. These communities did not know the other, that is, the neighbor, as an abstract, anonymous, and unknown member of category that was potentially incarnated in the face of anyone with no exceptions. This recognition occurred in the West in the centuries between the spread of the Judeo-Christian tradition and the democratic constitutions. Through the force of this awareness, concern for the excluded, for the victims of economic, social, environmental contradictions, came to be universally understood as just.

The historical origin of this attention toward those who are excluded and victims of any type and in any place is a famous parable, according to which we must take care of the persecuted other, even if the other is an enemy. It is the parable of the Good Samaritan. It tells of a man who comes across an unknown man who has been attacked by robbers, identifies with his condition, and takes time to dress his wounds fraternally and takes over the cost of his recovery.[18]

Recognizing in the Judeo-Christian revelation the principle of fraternity does not mean claiming the superiority for Judeo-Christian morality over other ideal motivations that sustain current political and cultural choices.[19] It means in fact accepting the historicity of the Judeo-Christian tradition as the roots of the modern principle of fraternity, as it is affirmed by the different ideal traditions that meet in the value of democracy.[20]

Freedom has a limit, and progress and economic growth have a limit; all these limits reside in the existence of the other and in recognition of the right of a person to exist as he or she is, which lies at the heart of a collectivity.

Commitment to a search for fraternity is an essential

condition for ensuring that the individualistic and competitive character of interpersonal relations in late-modern society does not degenerate into solipsistic and self-destructive behaviors, and for ensuring that ressentiment can evolve creatively, leading to critical movements, in full awareness of our interdependence with our neighbor, in new personal, professional, communicative, and political competences.

The experience of powerlessness that is typical of ressentiment can be transformed into a search for solidarity and fraternity: the suffering of ressentiment becomes the necessary step to the full realization that the comparison with the other is not only a source of humiliation, of rivalry, but also the space for solidarity and mutual interdependence. The desire to respond to violence thus becomes a desire to restore solidarity, and ressentiment—part of the response—instead of poisoning the soul becomes the soul's salvation.

We now know that it is no longer possible to imagine planning our future cohabitation on faith in technological progress and in technocratic systems that would gradually abolish antagonisms. If the mission of democratic anthropology, in a period when ressentiment increasingly intoxicates daily relationships, consists in enhancing the ability of men and women to recognize reciprocally their fragility and their mutual dependence, in turning disappointments generated by general competitive struggles into social criticism and into the construction of egalitarian and collaborative relationships, the spirit of fraternity must be rediscovered as the heart of this mission.

Conclusion

> What occupies me, and what I am qualified to
> speak about, is the victims of this Reich. I don't
> want to erect a monument to them, for to be a
> victim alone is not an honor. I only wanted to
> describe their condition, which is unchangeable.
>
> —Jean Améry, *At the Mind's Limits*

It is typical nowadays to interpret problems of social structures as if the solutions were up to the individual person.
As already claimed by C. Wright Mills back in the 1960s,
most problems of collective order can be traced back to the
framework of the individual's vital spaces and to face-to-face
interactions. The predominant orientation remains that of
providing a mainly psychological explanation for an entire

series of critical and contradictory situations of a systemic and structural nature. This "intimization" of social processes is so widespread in common sentiment that social players find it more and more difficult to imagine intersecting spaces between their private life and the great transformations taking place in historic and institutional scenarios.

In particular, if the specific case of affective life is considered, nowadays it seems that everything depends on the individual and his or her competences, abilities, personal aptitudes, and mostly close relationships. On the one hand, the effect of this flattening on the individual can be understood as resulting from the gap between individual biographies and the problems of social structures; on the other hand, it corresponds to the abandonment of subjects to solitude and the incapacity of critically examining the entire society in which they live.

There is, however, a very close bond between this feeling and great historic transformations, which, although hard to represent in contemporary collective imagination, continue even now to profoundly modify the life projects of social actors. The relational theory of ressentiment may be seen as an attempt to reconstitute this bond, which seems to be unraveling into an unbridgeable divide, even though in reality it is, as we shall see, the result of the social transformations that mark this difficult endemic crisis.

Today's crisis has various causes and more than one consequence at the social level. The disquiet generated by the spread of ressentiment heralds two aspects of the collapse of the system as a whole that are closely connected. On the one hand there is the dissipation of individual energy in interminable and sectorial competitions with outcomes that are increasingly hostile; on the other hand there is the greater inflexibility of democratic institutions, which were born in the recent modern period.

The first aspect is manifested in the frustration of people pursuing an unattainable goal that they at the same time feel they cannot forgo. Individuals live in mimetic situations, knowing that these often are very uncertain situations from which they cannot escape for fear of becoming outcasts. The result is a paralyzing anxiety, similar to what a person feels who is preparing for a test, the outcome of which (the fulfillment of the desire) depends on such a large number of variables (rivals) that there is no point in trying. The result is also great aggressiveness, a "rampant" attitude of aggressiveness that is considered to be the only suitable one for "winning" the competition.

The second aspect of this collapse is found in the progressive separation of the lives of ordinary people and the system of democratic institutions on the one hand, and, on the other, separation from the great technological-economic apparatuses. Subjectively, individuals feel increasingly that they are citizens of the world, but at the same time they feel isolated and powerless, part of a far and distant social system that is as large as the planet, but of which they know and control only a very small part. The problem is that they experience systemic contradictions very deeply, often in a disorienting manner and to their own personal cost: they are made redundant because their company has had to shut because of the global economic situation; they find it difficult to access the world of work; they face fierce competition; they are affected by war.

The analysis of ressentiment shows that it is possible to emerge from this crisis if we acknowledge the close relationship between the culture of democracy and ressentiment. The basic lines of this link are different from, although not entirely opposite to, those traced by Nietzsche. Today's image of ressentiment, which Nietzsche so brilliantly portrayed, is based on an idea of emotions as individual and private phenomena that exclude a priori the role of the other in our personal experiences, unless, it is thought, we are immature enough to be marked by the role of the other.

The main focus of a relational theory of ressentiment is to stress the intimately social and public warp and weft of our emotions and how closely they are tied up with the institutional order. Through the reconstruction of the notion of the scapegoat, of mimesis, of its relational configuration, a relational and social model of ressentiment is delineated. A lot of ground still needs to be covered in this direction, but I hope to have provided a sufficiently clear theoretical contribution. I will have succeeded if this book can lead to stimulating an effective critical discussion of crucial questions of our common life that are implicit in the modern image of ressentiment.

Democracy is part and parcel of an institutional setup that aims to acknowledge and at the same time to contain and regulate the ressentiment of people, without resorting to exclusion and expulsion, as was the case in archaic, mythical, and ritualistic institutional orders. Democracy, and with it the world of rights opened up by modernity, recognizes that every one of our affective experiences is profoundly ambivalent, and it grants each, ressentiment included, equal citizenship.

Our affective life takes shape from our natural condition of incompleteness, of unavoidable lack. Every human being opens up to the other owing to his or her intimate anthropological constitution even more than through a conscious moral choice. Our portrayal of ourselves and perception of ourselves through the other, our continuous and incessant comparisons with one another, give a deep sense of our affective experience, where all feeling is of necessity related to the feeling of others.

Our human fragility, contrary to what Nietzsche imagined, is the mark of this constitutional incompleteness, of this opening that enables us to feel and suffer, to experience emotions that never only reflect an inner world, but are joint enterprises in which several people participate together, enterprises that are part and parcel of the incessant construction of our social order, of our institutional and power relationships.

• • •

I must now take my leave. I shall do so by telling the story of a man who in his fragility, in his shortcomings, provided us with a glimpse of how human dignity can coexist with human baseness and through this exalt it.

It is the story of Jonah, who disobeys God and abandons his country and escapes to foreign lands. He wanders alone but carries with him the marks of his identity: he is a Jew. At the port, where he boards ship for Tarshish, the sailors recognize from his accent that he is not like them; his clothes, his manner, his gestures show that he belongs to a people that have never much loved the sea. But when he went on board Jonah threw in his lot with any other voyager who had linked his fate to that of the ship.

Once at sea, a strong wind blew up and the ensuing storm threatened to break up the ship. The crew was frantic; in the crisis hierarchy collapsed, differences were canceled. There was no longer any order on the ship but disorder created by the universal desire to survive. Of anyone who had experienced shipwreck, who would not now be prepared to kill in order to save his own life in return? Fear soon turns into mutual hatred, a painful anxiety that turns into the ressentiment of those who have the will to survive. The crew all share the same destiny, but paradoxically this identical fate divides them rather than it unites them. Anxiety feeds on the ressentiment of the survivor, turning everyone against everyone. Everyone is possessed by ressentiment.

There is nothing left but to cling to the last remaining certainty: they all call on their god. The mystery of the sacred is the only secure barrier to halt the panic that is spreading through the ship. But not even the pagan gods hear the men's cries of desperation. They do not listen, and not even Jonah listens to those cries. While the crew is gripped by the fear of death, he sleeps, remains alone for hours and hours, sleeping in a corner of the ship. He ignores the people around him; he wants only to sleep deeply. In the chaos of the storm, where nobody is recognizable any longer, hiding behind the mask of horror and hatred, the difference of which Jonah is the guardian is striking: indifference.

The captain of the ship finds that this indifference is a provocation: "Why are you sleeping like that! Get up and pray to your gods! God may take pity on us and we will not perish." "Let us draw lots," the crew cries, pointing at Jonah. "That way we will know who is the cause of this misfortune of ours." And chance picks out Jonah, because he is the victim of a bitter tautology: the chosen person will be condemned, because he is surely guilty. But on the ship nobody knows what wrong Jonah has done; nobody knows that he fled in order not to obey his God. For his persecutors, the fact that he did not pray is sufficient proof. Jonah must be the victim that is to be sacrificed in order to overcome the peril. It is no accident that once the guilty party has been revealed, the double face of the identity reemerges: "Tell us at least the cause of the evil that has befallen us; what do you do for a living? Where do you come from? What is your country and who are your people?"

"Seize me and throw me into the sea," cries Jonah. "The sea will become calm, because I know that this great storm has struck you because of me." But what wrong has this man done to his persecutors if they do not know the true reason, his disobeying God, and do not even believe in the same God?

Jonah's fate is now sealed, perhaps because of his pride, perhaps because of his disobedience, or also because of his indifference: he is guilty, condemned to ensure the survival of the community through his own death. At that precise moment, Jonah incarnates the metaphor of the Jewish people, the innocent victims of persecution.

Metaphor follows metaphor. Jonah survives. He is swallowed by a big fish and will return to terra firma after three days and three nights, carrying with him the founding murder, on which every social order is based: "From the belly of the abyss I cried," Jonah prays. "The waters closed around my soul, the abyss swallowed me and the algae clustered around my head." The subterranean desires of those men who were frantic to survive chased Jonah into the abyss; his sacrifice was necessary to calm the hatred and poison of those surrounding him. Just like those sailors on the ship, we all are also heirs to this murder: the risk of being caught up in the labyrinths of envy, of ressentiment, of hatred, is always present in all human relations.

So is it also with Jonah. Although he had suffered persecution, he does not hesitate to invoke vengeance when he reaches Nineveh. It is Jonah who proclaims God's wrath: "In forty days Nineveh shall be overturned." The citizens of Nineveh experience the fear that took hold of the ship's crew: the specter of death draws nigh. The king orders general fasting and everyone dons sackcloth and ashes. For the second time in the story of Jonah, a community is thrown into disarray, and there are no longer recognizable differences and hierarchies, not even between humans and animals: the king and his subjects, like all the animals in the city, fast and dress the same.

However, during this crisis, something extraordinary happens. The community of Nineveh does not choose a victim to sacrifice, but awaits God's forgiveness in silence. God sees repentance in their actions, the renunciation of violence and the process of sacrifice. Vengeance is replaced by forgiveness, which comes promptly. This, however, makes Jonah indignant; he takes issue with God, who has decided not to exact vengeance. Jonah even prefers death to the idea that God can forgive evil. Jonah is ensnared by ressentiment, by the pull of the desire for revenge that beats against the obstacle of forgiveness. Jonah is very angry with God and goes back to his source: "That is why I immediately fled to Tarshish, because I knew that you are a merciful God who is slow to anger, has great compassion, is completely benevolent, and is loath to punish. But now I beg you to take my soul from me because I prefer death to life."

But God does not take his life. Slow to anger, he gives him another chance to understand the difference between revenge and pardon. When Jonah falls asleep, God makes a castor oil plant grow up near him so that his head is shaded; at dawn God sends a worm to attack the roots and makes the plant dry up. Jonah again waxes indignant, caught up by presumption and by ressentiment of the offense inflicted by God. But God admonishes him, forcing him to reflect: "You took pity on the castor oil plant for which you did not work, which you did not grow, which grew in a night and was destroyed in a night. Should I not take pity on Nineveh, the large city in which more than six score thousand people live, who cannot tell their right hands from their left hands, in addition to the large number of animals?"

•   •   •

Perhaps nobody is able to escape from ressentiment, but the story of Jonah suggests a way. It reveals the alibis of ressentiment. When Jonah gets to Nineveh, he believes that he is one of the just, one of those who are victim of the injustices of others, and he confuses the desire for justice with his own ressentiment. When he then finds shade under the castor oil plant, he fools himself into thinking that he is a man who has finally overcome his own fragility. He thinks that he no longer needs to ask anyone for help and comfort. Nevertheless, as soon as the worm eats the roots of the plant, he finds himself exposed to the heat of the sun and again falls prey to the ressentiment of those who cannot bear depending on others. If there is a moral in the story of Jonah, I think it concerns human relationships. He confirms that a condition of mutual dependency exists that is characteristic of all human relationships: mimetism. It is a constituent part of the good and evil of our way of being. The story of Jonah shows that if this dependence on others is denied, it can be transformed into ressentiment. Denying the reality of mimetism, Girard would say, is one of the main causes of ressentiment. The story of Jonah suggests that one way of overcoming our ressentiment is to admit all this.

Notes

Foreword by Paul Dumouchel

1. Peter Strawson, "Freedom and Resentment," in *Perspectives on Moral Responsibility*, ed. J.M. Fischer and M. Ravizza (Ithaca: Cornell University Press, 1993), 45–66; originally published in *Proceedings of the British Academy 48* (1962), 1–25.

2. Ibid., 49.

Introduction

1. Friedrich Nietzsche, *The Genealogy of Morals*, trans. Horace Barnett Samuel (New York: Dover Publications, 2003).

2. Paul Dumouchel, *Émotions: Essai sur le corps et le social* (Paris: Les empêcheurs de penser en rond, 1995).

3. C. Wright Mills, *The Sociological Imagination* (Oxford:

Oxford University Press, 2000).

4. Erving Goffman, *Interaction Ritual: Essays on Face-to-Face Behavior* (Chicago: Aldine, 1967).

5. Max Scheler, *Ressentiment*, trans. William Holdheim, ed. Lewis A. Coser (New York: Schocken, 1972).

6. Richard Sachts, *Nietzsche, Genealogy, Morality: Essays on Nietzsche's* On the Genealogy of Morals (Berkeley: University of California Press, 1994).

7. Gilles Deleuze, *Nietzsche and Philosophy*, trans. Hugh Tomlinson (New York: Columbia University Press, 1983).

8. René Girard, "Dionysus versus the Crucified," *MLN* 99, no. 4 (September 1984): 816–35.

9. See the studies of Jack M. Barbalet, *Emotion, Social Theory, and Social Structure: A Macrosociological Approach* (Cambridge: Cambridge University Press, 1998); Marc Ferro, *Resentment in History* (Cambridge, UK: Polity Press, 2010); Bernardino Fantini, Dolores Martín Moruno, and Javier Moscoso, eds., *On Resentment: Past and Present* (Cambridge, UK: Cambridge Scholars Publishing, 2013).

10. Wolfang Palaver, *René Girard's Mimetic Theory*, trans. Gabriel Borrud (East Lansing: Michigan State University

Press, 2013).

11. René Girard, *Il risentimento*, ed. Stefano Tomelleri (Milan: Raffaello Cortina, 1999).

12. Jean-Pierre Dupuy and Paul Dumouchel, *L'énfer des choses: René Girard et la logique de l'économie* (Paris: Seuil, 1979).

13. Émile Durkheim, *The Elementary Forms of Religious Life*, trans. Carol Cosman (Oxford: Oxford University Press, 2001).

14. Dumouchel, *Émotions*, esp. ch. 1.

15. Richard Sennett, *The Culture of the New Capitalism* (New Haven, CT: Yale University Press, 2006).

16. Anthony Giddens, *The Transformation of Intimacy: Sexuality, Love and Eroticism in Modern Societies* (Cambridge, UK: Polity Press, 1992).

Chapter 1. The Revolt of the Slaves at the Masters' Banquet

1. Friedrich Nietzsche, *The Genealogy of Morals*, trans. Horace Barnett Samuel (New York: Dover Publications, 2003), 5.

2. Deleuze, *Nietzsche and Philosophy*.

3. As we shall see more fully later on, in *Nietzsche and*

Philosophy, Deleuze places the idea of the reactive force of ressentiment at the center of his interpretation of Nietzsche's thought.

4. Sergio Moravia, "Morale come dominio," introduction to Friedrich Nietzsche, *La genealogia della morale*, ed. Moravia (Rome: Newton & Compton, 1993), i–x.

5. For the *prototypes* in Nietzsche's philosophy as set out in *The Genealogy of Morals*, see "La genealogia della morale nell'opera di Nietzsche," the study that Sossio Giametta presents in the introduction to the Italian edition, *La genealogia della morale*, ed. Giametta (Milan: BUR, 1997).

6. Giametta, "La genealogia della morale," 10.

7. Nietzsche, *The Genealogy of Morals*, 21.

8. Ibid.

9. Ibid., 47.

10. Friedrich Nietzsche, *The Anti-Christ, Ecce Homo, Twilight of the Gods and Other Writings* (Cambridge: Cambridge University Press, 2005), 164.

11. See the studies of the historians Jean-Pierre Vernant and Pierre Vidal-Naquet, *Mythe et tragédie en Grèce ancienne* (Paris: Librairie François Maspero, 1972) on the transition

from the mythological order to the legal order in ancient Greece.

12. Gianni Vattimo, *Il soggetto e la maschera* (Milan: Bompiani, 1974), 43–68.

13. Vernant and Vidal-Naquet, *Mythe et tragédie*.

14. Nietzsche, *The Genealogy of Morals*, 19.

15. Deleuze's essay is linked to the hermeneutic-linguistic interpretive trend that was particularly popular in France in the 1960s and 1970s and that placed at the center of its research the theme of genealogy as a descriptive deconstruction of the logical-linguistic structures of metaphysics. For a detailed analysis of these readings of Nietzsche, see Vattimo, *Il soggetto e la maschera*, which is dedicated to the themes of the subject and of the mask in the works of Nietzsche.

Chapter 2. Bourgeois Philanthropy

1. Scheler, *Ressentiment*, 81–82.

2. Scheler's position here was greatly influenced by the work of Werner Sombart, *The Jews and Modern Capitalism*, trans. Mortimer Epstein (London: Unwin, 1913). See

Patrik Lang, "Max Scheler's Analysis of *Ressentiment* in Modern Democracies," in *On Resentment*, 55–70.

3. For an in-depth analysis of the modern weltanschauung in Scheler's work, see Gianfranco Morra's studies. Morra identified four essential features of this weltanschauung: (1) the separation of the individual from the conscious unity of the other: God, nature, man become antithetical entities; (2) the triumph of the capitalist ethos (unlimited work impulse and consequently an unlimited acquisitive impulse); (3) predominance of ressentiment and of mistrust: reduction of gemeinschaft to gesellschaft; (4) prevalence of the mathematical-mechanistic explanation; see Gianfranco Morra, "Ethos borghese e rinascimento nell'interpretazione di Max Scheler," *Ethica* 11, no. 3 (1972): 222–23.

4. Scheler, *Ressentiment*, 143.

5. Angelo Pupi, "Introduzione," in *Il risentimento nell'edificazione delle morali*, by Max Scheler (Milan: Vita e Pensiero, 1975), 5–11.

6. Scheler, *Ressentiment*, 45.

7. Ibid., 46.

8. Ibid., 68.

9. Ibid., 54.

10. Ibid., 48.

11. Ibid., 70–71.

12. For the English translation of this title, see Max Scheler, *The Nature of Sympathy*, trans. Peter Heath (New York: Archon Books, 1970).

13. As Angelo Pupi has remarked: "Life and power are the values that are implicit in Scheler's psychological analysis: and as these figures are not phenomena, it must be concluded that the author's considerations are based on a vitalistic philosophy that is not unlike Nietzsche's" (Pupi, "Introduzione," 14).

14. Roberto Esposito expresses the same opinion in his discussion of Jean Améry's "sociological" reading of ressentiment in Nietzsche and Scheler. See Roberto Esposito, "L'etica del risentimento," *Micromega* 2 (1988): 218–20.

Chapter 3. The Surprise Box of Ressentiment

1. Theodor W. Adorno, *Philosophische Terminologie* (Frankfurt am Main: Suhrkamp, 1973).

2. Jürgen Habermas, *Erkenntnis und Interesse* (Frankfurt am Main: Suhrkamp, 1968). For an in-depth analysis of the deconstructionist role played in modern and contemporary culture by Nietzsche's works in general and by *The Genealogy of Morals* in particular, see the studies of Nietzsche by Vattimo, *Il soggetto e la maschera*.

3. Scheler, *Ressentiment*, 59.

4. Nietzsche, *The Genealogy of Morals*, 84.

5. Scheler, *Ressentiment*, 172.

6. Norberto Bobbio, *Teoria generale della politica* (Turin: Einaudi, 1999).

7. Primo Levi, *The Drowned and the Saved*, trans. Raymond Rosenthal (New York: Vintage, 1989), 36–37.

Chapter 4. The Last of the Scapegoats

1. There has been increasing interest in this author in recent years in Italy, and this has been reflected in original works on Girard and the many later studies dedicated

to his theoretical reflections. A complete and exhaustive bibliography of all the writings of and on René Girard can be found in the Girard-Dokumentation of the Faculty of Theology of the University of Innsbruck.

2. For the subsequent theoretical reworkings, see the documentation cited in the previous note. In particular, see Dupuy and Dumouchel, *L'enfer des choses*; Paul Dumouchel, "Différences et paradoxes: Réflexions sur l'amour et la violence dans l'ouvre de Girard," in *René Girard et le problème du mal*, ed. Michel Deguy and Jean-Pierre Dupuy (Paris: Édition Grasset & Fasquelle, 1972), 215–23; Jean-Pierre Dupuy, *Ordres et désordres* (Paris: Seuil, 1982); Stefano Tomelleri, *René Girard: La matrice sociale della violenza* (Milan: Franco Angeli, 2000).

3. Sigmund Freud, *Totem und Tabu* (Hamburg: Duncker & Humblot, 1912).

4. René Girard, *Violence and the Sacred*, trans. Patrick Gregory (Baltimore: Johns Hopkins University Press, 1977), 93.

5. Paul Valadier, "Violenza del sacro e non violenza del cristianesimo nel pensiero di René Girard," *La civiltà*

cattolica 134 (1983): 365.

6. René Girard, *The Scapegoat*, trans. Yvonne Freccero (Baltimore: Johns Hopkins University Press, 1986), 44.

7. See, inter alia, Paul Ricoeur, "Religion and Symbolic Violence," *Contagion* 6 (1999): 7–18.

8. René Girard, *Things Hidden since the Foundation of the World: Research Undertaken in Collaboration with J. M. Oughourlian and G. Lefort*, trans. Stephen Bann and Micheal Metteer (Stanford, CA: Stanford University Press, 1987).

9. For more information on the relationship between revenge and the sacrificial system in Girard's mimetic theory, see the study of Mark R. Anspach, *À charge de revanche* (Paris: Seuil, 2002).

10. Girard, *The Scapegoat*, 101.

11. Gianni Vattimo and René Girard, *Christianity, Truth, and Weakening Faith: A Dialogue*, trans. David William McCuaig (New York: Columbia University Press, 2010).

12. Girard, *Il risentimento*, xi.

13. Girard, *Violence and the Sacred*, 205.

14. René Girard, *Deceit, Desire, and the Novel: Self and Other*

in Literary Structure, trans. Yvonne Freccero (Baltimore: Johns Hopkins University Press, 1966).

15. René Girard, "The Founding Murder in the Philosophy of Nietzsche," in *Violence and Truth: On the Work of René Girard*, ed. Paul Dumouchel (Stanford, CA: Stanford University Press, 1988), 227–46.

16. Girard, "Dionysius versus the Crucified," *Modern Language Notes* 92, (1977), 1175.

17. Girard's position here is in some ways close to that of Max Scheler. But unlike Scheler, Girard also challenges the very premises of the Nietzschean model of ressentiment, whereas Scheler, as we have seen, accepts them all, if only to turn them against Nietzsche.

Chapter 5. The Mimetic Nature of Our Ressentiment

1. See Dupuy and Dumouchel, *L'enfer des choses*.

2. Gabriel Tarde, *Les lois de l'imitation: Étude sociologique* (Paris: Felix Alcan Éditeur, 1890).

3. Girard, *Il risentimento*, x.

4. Jean-Pierre Dupuy, *Le sacrifice et l'envie* (Paris: Calmann-Lévy, 1992), 115–25.

5. For information on the link between the thought of Gregory Bateson and Girard's mimetic theory, see the studies of Simon Simonse, *Kings of Disaster: Dualism, Centralism, and the Scapegoat King in Southeastern Sudan* (Leiden: Brill, 1992) and Sergio Manghi, *La conoscenza ecologica* (Milan: Raffaello Cortina, 2004), 60–75.

6. Dupuy and Dumouchel, *L'enfer des choses*.

7. Girard, *Il risentimento*.

8. Dupuy, *Le sacrifice et l'envie*.

9. Arnold Ghelen, *Der Mensch: Seine Natur und seine Stellung in der Welt* (Bonn: Athenäum-Verlag, 1950).

10. René Girard, *I See Satan Fall Like Lightning*, trans. James G. Williams (Maryknoll, NY: Orbis Books, 2001).

Chapter 6. Toward a Sociology of Ressentiment

1. The English edition of this book is *Deceit, Desire, and the Novel: Self and Other in Literary Structure* (1966).

2. René Girard, "Superman in the Underground: Strategies of Madness: Nietzsche, Wagner and Dostoevsky," *Modern Language Notes* 91 (1976): 1161–85; Girard, *I See Satan Fall*, 161–69.

3. Ivan Illich, *Œuvres complètes*, vol. 1 (Paris: Fayard, 2004).

4. William Blake Tyrrell, *The Sacrifice of Socrates: Athens, Plato, Girard* (East Lansing: Michigan State University Press, 2012).

5. Girard, *Things Hidden*.

6. Paul Dumouchel, *Le sacrifice inutile* (Paris: Flammarion, 2011); *The Barren Sacrifice*, tr. Mary Baker (East Lansing: Michigan State University Press, 2015).

7. Marcel Detienne, *Comment être autochtone?* (Paris: Seuil, 2003).

8. Antonio Gramsci, *La questione meridionale* (Rome: Editori Riuniti, 1966).

9. Lynda De Matteo, *L'idiota in politica* (Milan: Feltrinelli, 2011).

10. Ernesto Laclau, *On Populist Reason* (London: Verso, 2005).

11. Mauro Magatti and Mario De Benedittis, *I nuovi ceti popolari: Chi ha preso il posto della classe operaia* (Milan: Feltrinelli, 2006).

12. Aldo Bonomi, *Il capitalismo molecolare: La società al lavoro nel Nord Italia* (Turin: Einaudi, 1997).

13. Aldo Bonomi, *Il rancore: Alle radici del malessere del nord* (Milan: Fetrinelli, 2008).

14. Giampiero Rossi and Simone Spina, *Lo spaccone: L'incredibile storia di Umberto Bossi il padrone della Lega* (Rome: Editori Riuniti, 2004).

15. "Mani Pulite" means "clean hands."

16. Antonio Di Pietro, *Intervista su mani pulite* (Rome: Laterza, 2000).

17. Robert Castel, *L'insécurité sociale: Qu'est-ce qu'être protégé?* (Paris: Seuil, 2003).

18. Manuel Castells and Pekka Himanen, *The Information Society and the Welfare State: The Finnish Model* (Oxford: Oxford University Press, 2002).

19. Steve Fuller, *The New Sociological Imagination* (London: Sage, 2006).

20. Wolfang Palaver, "A Girardian Reading of Schmitt's Political Theology," *Telos* 93 (1992): 43–68.

21. Richard Sennett, *The Fall of Public Man* (New York: Alfred A. Knopf, 1977).

22. Mauro Magatti, *Libertà immaginaria: Le illusioni del capitalismo tecno-nichilista* (Milan: Feltrinelli, 2009).

23. Elenonora Bianchini, *Il libro che la Lega Nord non ti farebbe mai leggere* (Rome: Newton Compton Editori, 2010).

Chapter 7. From Victim-Playing to the Ethics of Ressentiment

1. Paul Dumouchel, "A Mimetic Rereading of Helmut Shoeck's Theory of Envy," in *Passions in Economy, Politics, and the Media: In Discussion with Christian Theology*, ed. Wolfgang Palaver and Petra Steinmair-Posël (Vienna: LIT Verlag, 2005); see Dumouchel, *The Ambivalence of Scarcity and Other Essays* (East Lansing: Michigan State University Press, 2014), 109–25.

2. Miguel Benasayag and Gérard Schmit, *Les passions tristes: Souffrance physique et crise sociale* (Paris: La Découverte, 2006).

3. Bert van den Brink and David Owen, *Recognition and Power: Axel Honneth and the Tradition of Critical Social Theory* (Cambridge: Cambridge University Press, 2007).

4. Alain Touraine, *Le retour de l'acteur: Essai de sociologie* (Paris: Fayard, 1984).

5. Esposito, "L'etica del risentimento," 218.

6. Jean Améry, *At the Mind's Limits: Contemplations by a Survivor on Auschwitz and Its Realities*, trans. Sidney Rosenfeld and Stella P. Rosenfeld (New York: Schocken,

1986), x.

7. Everett L. Worthington Jr., ed., *Handbook of Forgiveness* (New York: Brunner-Routledge, 2005).

8. Etienne Mullet, Fèlix Neto, and Sebastian Rivière, "Personality and Its Effects on Resentment, Revenge, Forgiveness, and Self-Forgiveness," in *Handbook of Forgiveness*, ed. Everett L. Worthington Jr. (New York: Brunner-Routledge, 2005), 159–82.

9. Edgar Morin, *La connaissance de la connaissance* (Paris: Seuil, 1986).

10. Dumouchel, *The Barren Sacrifice*.

11. Zygmunt Bauman, *The Individualized Society* (Cambridge, UK: Polity Press, 2001).

12. Magatti, *Libertà immaginaria*.

13. Kristen Renwick Monroe, *The Heart of Altruism: Perceptions of a Common Humanity* (Princeton, NJ: Princeton University Press, 1998); Sergio Manghi, "Altruismo," *Rassegna Italiana di Sociologia* 3 (1995): 433–59; and Sergio Manghi, *Il soggetto ecologico di Edgar Morin: Verso una società-mondo* (Trento: Erickson, 2009).

14. Sergio Manghi, "Nessuno escluso," *Pluriverso* 4–5 (1999): 204–18.

15. Adriano Zamperini, *Psicologia dell'inerzia e della solidarietà: Il ruolo degli spettatori nelle atrocità collettive* (Turin: Einaudi, 2001).

16. Filippo Pizzolato, *Il principio costituzionale di fraternità: Itinerario di ricerca a partire dalla Costituzione italiana* (Rome: Città Nuova, 2012).

17. John Rawls, *A Theory of Justice* (Cambridge, MA: Harvard University Press, 1971).

18. Michel Borgetto, *La devise "Libertè, Égalitè, Fraternitè"* (Paris: Presses Universitaires de France, 1997).

19. James G. Williams, "The Sermon on the Mount as a Christian Basis of Altruism," *Humboldt Journal of Social Relations* 13, nos. 1–2 (1985–86): 89–112.

20. René Girard, *Battling to the End: Conversation with Benoît Chantre*, trans. Mary Baker (East Lansing: Michigan State University Press, 2010).

Bibliography

Adorno, Theodor W. *Philosophische Terminologie.* Frankfurt am Main: Suhrkamp, 1973.

Alberoni, Francesco. *Genesi.* Milan: Garzanti, 1989.

Améry, Jean. *At the Mind's Limits: Contemplations by a Survivor on Auschwitz and Its Realities.* Translated by Sidney Rosenfeld and Stella P. Rosenfeld. New York: Schocken, 1986.

Anspach, Mark R. *À charge de revanche.* Paris: Seuil, 2002.

Barbalet, Jack M. *Emotion, Social Theory, and Social Structure: A Macrosociological Approach.* Cambridge: Cambridge University Press, 1998.

Bauman, Zygmunt. *The Individualized Society.* Cambridge, UK: Polity Press, 2001.

———. *Liquid Modernity.* Cambridge, UK: Polity Press, 2000.

Benasayag, Miguel, and Gérard Schmit. *Les passions tristes: Souffrance physique et crise sociale.* Paris: La Découverte, 2006.

Bianchini, Elenonora. *Il libro che la Lega Nord non ti farebbe mai leggere.* Rome: Newton Compton Editori, 2010.

Bobbio, Norberto. *Teoria generale della politica.* Turin: Einaudi, 1999.

Bonomi, Aldo. *Il capitalismo molecolare: La società al lavoro nel Nord Italia.* Turin: Einaudi, 1997.

——— . *Il rancore: Alle radici del malessere del nord.* Milan: Fetrinelli, 2008.

Borgetto, Michel. *La devise "Liberté, Égalité, Fraternité."* Paris: Presses Universitaires de France, 1997.

Castel, Robert. *L'insécurité sociale: Qu'est-ce qu'être protégé?* Paris: Seuil, 2003.

Castells, Manuel, and Pekka Himanen. *The Information Society and the Welfare State: The Finnish Model.* Oxford: Oxford University Press, 2002.

Deleuze, Gilles. *Nietzsche and Philosophy.* Translated by Hugh Tomlinson. New York: Columbia University Press, 1983.

De Matteo, Lynda. *L'idiota in politica.* Milan: La Feltrinelli, 2011.

Detienne, Marcel. *Comment être autochtone?* Paris: Seuil, 2003.

Di Pietro, Antonio. *Intervista su mani pulite*. Rome: Laterza, 2000.

Dumouchel, Paul. *The Ambivalence of Scarcity and Other Essays*. East Lansing: Michigan State University Press, 2014.

———. *The Barren Sacrifice*, tr. Mary Baker East Lansing: Michigan State University Press, 2015.

———. "Différences et paradoxes: Réflexions sur l'amour et la violence dans l'ouvre de Girard." In *René Girard et le problème du mal*, edited by Michel Deguy and Jean-Pierre Dupuy, 215–23. Paris: Édition Grasset & Fasquelle, 1972.

———. *Émotions: Essaisur le corps et le social*. Paris: Les empêcheurs de penser en rond, 1995.

———. *Le sacrifice inutile*. Paris: Flammarion, 2011.

———. "A Mimetic Rereading of Helmut Shoeck's Theory of Envy," in *Passions in Economy, Politics, and the Media: In Discussion with Christian Theology*, edited by Wolfang Palaver and Petra Steinmair-Posël, 103–22. Vienna: LIT Verlag, 2005.

Dupuy, Jean-Pierre. *Le sacrifice et l'envie*. Paris: Calmann-Lévy, 1992.

———. *Ordres et désordres.* Paris: Seuil, 1982.

Dupuy, Jean-Pierre, and Paul Dumouchel. *L'énfer des choses: René Girard et la logique de l'économie.* Paris: Seuil, 1979.

Durkheim, Émile. *The Elementary Forms of Religious Life.* Translated by Carol Cosman. Oxford: Oxford University Press, 2001.

Esposito, Roberto. "L'etica del risentimento." *Micromega* 2 (1988): 218–20.

Fantini, Bernardino, Dolores Martín Moruno, and Javier Moscoso, eds. *On Resentment: Past and Present.* Cambridge, UK: Cambridge Scholars Publishing, 2013.

Ferro, Marc. *Resentment in History.* Cambridge, UK: Polity Press, 2010.

Freud, Sigmund. *Totem und Tabu.* Hamburg: Duncker & Humblot, 1912.

Fuller, Steve. *The New Sociological Imagination.* London: Sage, 2006.

Ghelen, Arnold. *Der Mensch: Seine Natur und seine Stellung in der Welt.* Bonn: Athenäum-Verlag, 1950.

Giametta, Sossio. "La genealogia della morale nell'opera di Nietzsche." In *La genealogia della morale*, by Friedrich

Nietzsche and edited by Sossio Giametta, 5–31. Milan: BUR, 1997.

———. *Nietzsche: Il poeta, il moralista, il filosofo.* Milan: Garzanti, 1991.

Giddens, Anthony. *The Transformation of Intimacy: Sexuality, Love and Eroticism in Modern Societies.* Cambridge, UK: Polity Press, 1992.

Girard, René. *Battling to the End: Conversation with Benoît Chantre.* Translated by Mary Baker. East Lansing: Michigan State University Press, 2010.

———. *Deceit, Desire, and the Novel: Self and Other in Literary Structure.* Translated by Yvonne Freccero. Baltimore: Johns Hopkins University Press, 1966.

———. "Dionysus versus the Crucified." *MLN* 99, no. 4 (September 1984): 816–35.

———. "The Founding Murder in the Philosophy of Nietzsche." In *Violence and Truth: On the Work of René Girard*, edited by Paul Dumouchel, 227–46. Stanford, CA: Stanford University Press, 1988.

———. *Il risentimento.* Edited by Stefano Tomelleri. Milan: Raffaello Cortina, 1999.

———. *I See Satan Fall Like Lightning.* Translated by James G. Williams. Maryknoll, NY: Orbis Books, 2001.

———. *The Scapegoat.* Translated by Yvonne Freccero. Baltimore: Johns Hopkins University Press 1986.

———. "Superman in the Underground: Strategies of Madness: Nietzsche, Wagner and Dostoevsky," *MLN* 91, no. 6 (December 1976): 1161–85.

———. *Things Hidden since the Foundation of the World: Research Undertaken in Collaboration with J. M. Oughourlian and G. Lefort.* Translated by Stephen Bann and Micheal Metteer. Stanford, CA: Stanford University Press, 1987.

———. *Violence and the Sacred.* Translated by Patrick Gregory. Baltimore: Johns Hopkins University Press, 1977.

Goffman, Erving. *Interaction Ritual: Essays on Face-to-Face Behavior.* Chicago: Aldine, 1967.

Gramsci, Antonio. *La questione meridionale.* Rome: Editori Riuniti, 1966.

Grandjean, Antoine, and Florent Guénard. *Le ressentiment, passion sociale.* Rennes: Publication Universitaire De Rennes, 2012.

Habermas, Jürgen. *Erkenntnis und Interesse.* Frankfurt am Main: Suhrkamp, 1968.

Illich, Ivan. *Œuvres complètes.* Vol. 1. Paris: Fayard, 2004.

Laclau, Ernesto. *On Populist Reason.* London: Verso, 2005.

Levi, Primo. *The Drowned and the Saved.* Translated by Raymond Rosenthal. New York: Vintage, 1989.

Magatti, Mauro. *Libertà immaginaria: Le illusioni del capitalismo tecno-nichilista.* Milan: Feltrinelli, 2009.

Magatti, Mauro, and Mario De Benedittis. *I nuovi ceti popolari: Chi ha preso il posto della classe operaia.* Milan: Feltrinelli, 2006.

Manghi, Sergio. "Altruismo." *Rassegna Italiana di Sociologia* 3 (1995): 433–59.

——— . *Il soggetto ecologico di Edgar Morin: Verso una società-mondo.* Trento: Erickson, 2009.

——— . *La conoscenza ecologica.* Milan: Raffaello Cortina, 2004.

——— . "Nessuno escluso." *Pluriverso* 4–5 (1999): 204–18.

Mills, C. Wright. *The Sociological Imagination.* Oxford: Oxford University Press, 2000.

Monroe, Kristen Renwick. *The Heart of Altruism: Perceptions of a Common Humanity.* Princeton, NJ: Princeton University

Press, 1998.

Moravia, Sergio. "Morale come dominio." In *La genealogia della morale*, by Friedrich Nietzsche and edited by Sergio Moravia, i–x. Rome: Newton & Compton, 1993.

Morin, Edgar. *La connaissance de la connaissance*. Paris: Seuil, 1986.

Morra, Gianfranco. "Ethos borghese e rinascimento nell'interpretazione di Max Scheler." *Ethica* 11, no. 3 (1972): 220–30.

Mullet, Etienne, Fèlix Neto, and Sebastian Rivière. "Personality and Its Effects on Resentment, Revenge, Forgiveness, and Self-Forgiveness." In *Handbook of Forgiveness*, edited by Everett L. Worthington Jr., 159–82. New York: Brunner-Routledge, 2005.

Nietzsche, Friedrich. *The Anti-Christ, Ecce Homo, Twilight of the Gods and Other Writings*. Cambridge: Cambridge University Press, 2005.

———. *The Genealogy of Morals*. Translated by Horace Barnett Samuel. New York: Dover Publications, 2003.

Palaver, Wolfgang. "A Girardian Reading of Schmitt's Political Theology." *Telos* 93 (1992): 43–68.

———. *René Girard's Mimetic Theory.* Translated by Gabriel
    Borrud. East Lansing: Michigan State University Press,
    2013.

Pizzolato, Filippo. *Il principio costituzionale di fraternità:*
    Itinerario di ricerca a partire dalla Costituzione italiana.
    Rome: Città Nuova, 2012.

Pupi, Angelo. "Introduzione." In *Il risentimento edificazione delle*
    morali, by Max Scheler, 5–11. Milan: Vita e Pensiero, 1975.

Rawls, John. *A Theory of Justice.* Cambridge, MA: Harvard
    University Press, 1971.

Ricoeur, Paul. "Religion and Symbolic Violence." *Contagion* 6
    (1999): 7–18.

Rossi, Giampiero, and Simone Spina. *Lo spaccone: L'incredibile*
    storia di Umberto Bossi il padrone della Lega. Rome: Editori
    Riuniti, 2004.

Sachts, Richard. *Nietzsche, Genealogy, Morality: Essays on*
    Nietzsche's On the Genealogy of Morals. Berkeley:
    University of California Press, 1994.

Scheler, Max. *Ressentiment.* Translated by William Holdheim.
    Edited by Lewis A. Coser. New York: Schocken, 1972.

———. *Wesen und Formen der Sympathie.* Bern: Francke Verlag,

1922.

Sennett, Richard. *The Culture of the New Capitalism*. New Haven, CT: Yale University Press, 2006.

———. *The Fall of Public Man*. New York: Alfred A. Knopf, 1977.

———. *Together: The Rituals, Pleasures, and Politics of Cooperation*. New Haven: Yale University Press, 2012.

Schwager, Raymond. *Brauchen wir einen Sündenbock*. Munich: Kösel, 1978.

Simonse, Simon. *Kings of Disaster: Dualism, Centralism, and the Scapegoat King in Southeastern Sudan*. Leiden: Brill, 1992.

Sombart, Werner. *The Jews and Modern Capitalism*. Translated by Mortimer Epstein. London: Unwin, 1913.

Strawson, Peter. "Freedom and Resentment." In *Perspectives on Moral Responsibility*, edited by John M. Fischer and Mark Ravizza, 45–66. Ithaca: Cornell University Press, 1993.

Tarde, Gabriel. *Les lois de l'imitation: Étude sociologique*. Paris: Felix Alcan Éditeur, 1890.

Tomelleri, Stefano. *René Girard: La matrice sociale della violenza*. Milan: Franco Angeli, 2000.

Touraine, Alain. *Le retour de l'acteur: Essai de sociologie*. Paris:

Fayard, 1984.

Tyrrell, William Blake. *The Sacrifice of Socrates: Athens, Plato, Girard.* East Lansing: Michigan State University Press, 2012.

Valadier, Paul. "Violenza del sacro e non violenza del cristianesimo nel pensiero di René Girard." *La civiltà cattolica* 134 (1983): 350–65.

van den Brink, Bert, and David Owen, eds. *Recognition and Power: Axel Honneth and the Tradition of Critical Social Theory.* Cambridge: Cambridge University Press, 2007.

Vattimo, Gianni. *Il soggetto e la maschera.* Milan: Bompiani, 1974.

Vattimo, Gianni, and René Girard. *Christianity, Truth, and Weakening Faith: A Dialogue.* Translated by David William McCuaig. New York: Columbia University Press, 2010.

Vernant, Jean-Pierre, and Pierre Vidal-Naquet. *Mythe et tragédie en Grèce ancienne.* Paris: Librairie François Maspero, 1972.

Williams, James G. "The Sermon on the Mount as a Christian Basis of Altruism." *Humboldt Journal of Social Relations* 13, nos. 1–2 (1985–86): 89–112.

Worthington, Everett L., Jr., ed. *Handbook of Forgiveness.* New

York: Brunner-Routledge, 2005.

Zamperini, Adriano. *Psicologia dell'inerzia e della solidarietà: Il ruolo degli spettatori nelle atrocità collettive.* Turin: Einaudi, 2001.

Index